BACK TO BRIGHTON

Return To That Lovely Shore

by

Leonard Goldman

Published by

Leonard Goldman
26 Westfield Crescent
BRIGHTON
BN1 8JB

Printed by *digaprint*

Unit Two

54 Hollingdean Rd.
BRIGHTON BN2 4AA

ISBN 0 9530593 5 9

ACKNOWLEDGEMENTS

As will be seen, I have written and published these memoirs myself. But that bald statement can be misleading. Not a word could have been published nor the final script made printable and (I hope) readable without the help of many friends. My wife has been right through the story and suggested a whole number, not just of useful but of essential changes. She has also been the soul of restraint when work on the book has occupied my whole attention for long periods. Julia McGirr has again been a tower of strength with her superb and incisive editing. Chris Jones, with his vast store of IT know-how, has again and again been my saviour when all seemed lost. Michael Hayler, the originator of the whole project, has stood at my right hand when it came to setting up the copy for the printer and much else. I must also mention my brother-in-law, Reuben Falber, who gave me a unique insight into certain Party political developments and saved me from what could have been embarrassing misstatements. To all of these I offer my sincere gratitude. They must take their share of the credit for any successes the books have achieved but, I hasten to add, I take full responsibility for any lacks or failures. This might also be the appropriate place to thank my printers, *digaprint*, for their unfailing technical help and, as must be obvious, the outstanding job they have made of the physical production of the book. In that respect, it stands comparison with the most advanced professional productions.

CONTENTS

For Rita, Fleur, Tony, Poppy and Sasha, with all my love, in the hope that this concluding episode in my memoirs will interest and, perhaps, enlighten them.

INTRODUCTION

This is the third volume of my autobiography. The first was *Oh What a Lovely Shore*, in which I described my early childhood in various parts of the country and my schooldays in Brighton, the influence of a charismatic teacher, encouraging my interest in language, poetry and drama, as well as football, for which I was the school team's captain. I also wrote of the sea front and all its delights, the two piers, the magnificent hotels, resplendent in what seemed like permanent sunshine. From spring to autumn the beach was my second home and the delights of ploughing through the sea, in all its moods, never waned. I also mentioned that I started work as a shop assistant at the age of fourteen and referred to my engagement with left politics.

The second volume, *Brighton Beach to Bengal Bay*, dealt with the move to London and all the political, cultural and social turmoil of the tumultuous Thirties and recorded my membership of Unity Theatre and the Left Book Club. My friends and relations and all the influences they had on my life were also described in some detail, as was my four-year stint in a large West End store and my subsequent period as a commercial traveller, for Mars Confections Ltd.

Then came the war and a stay in Birmingham where I worked for my father and met a girl who I was to marry before being sent abroad, after a training period in the army. The destination was India where I spent four eventful and educative years, meeting many like-minded servicemen and getting to know a remarkable Bengali family. The book ends soon after VJ Day, and sees me on my way home to Blighty.

Both books met with some public acclaim and so I decided to continue and finalise the story...

EMBARKATION AND HOMECOMING

Unfortunately, I'd had no opportunity to say goodbye to my many Calcutta friends before I departed, as they were all away on holiday, so I left Howrah Station unaccompanied and entered the train with no fond farewells ringing in my ears. As we steamed noisily across the broad central plains, I took my last long look at the waterlogged rice paddies and palm-strewn fields, sweltering in fierce heat, a heat we experienced in our carriages too. For there were many others bound for Blighty on that train.

After a short stay in a camp not too far from Bombay, in which I met Arthur (of whom more later) we arrived in the relative cool of the evening and boarded the boat which was to carry us on the long voyage home. On the way out, we'd had to circumnavigate Africa, as the Mediterranean was "an Italian lake". With the end of the war, however, freedom of passage was restored for all and so we would be able to take the short route via the Suez Canal.

It is difficult, now, some fifty-seven years later, to recall my thoughts and feelings as I settled down to contemplate what lay before me. The dream of home, in all servicemen's thoughts from the day they embarked for abroad, was now turning into a reality. My wife, my parents and sisters, the green fields of England: it was hard to grasp this reality. It still seemed remote and dreamlike; indeed, I pushed it to the back of my mind and prepared to savour the delights, if any, of the voyage.

My closest companion on board was Arthur, the chap I had met en route to Bombay. He was tall, well over six feet, blonde and good looking in a conventional way and had undergone a course of body-building with an expert in Bombay, where he had been stationed for most of the time (lucky chap!). He was inordinately proud of his physique, bared his chest as often as possible and was always flexing his muscles. But he had intellectual longings, too.

He'd made a habit of writing down any word he encountered whose meaning he did not know and then looking it up in a dictionary he always carried with him. He had amassed quite a vocabulary in this way. He frequently read words to me from his list and was somewhat surprised, perhaps impressed, that I was acquainted with them and understood their use. On my side, I admired his tenacity.

8

We had one unfortunate quarrel during the voyage, when he became quite truculent, but this may have had something to do with the interminable lime marmalade we were ingesting at the time! On the whole, however, we grew to like each other and this friendship certainly made our trip less boring. We confided in each other and thus we each knew a great deal of the other's background and experiences. He or his friends are unlikely to read this (he may be dead by now he was, after all, about my age!) so I can reveal that, although happily married to a very attractive woman (I saw a photograph) he'd had an affair with a married woman in Bombay and regaled me with the details.

The passage through the Suez Canal had a certain fascination; we seemed in a world of our own, confined to this narrow strip of water. We leaned on the rail and watched as the artificial waves caused by the ship gradually surged right up to the canal side and lapped over on to the path that ran along the margin.

There were other interesting servicemen aboard. I remember two of them very well. One often described his schooldays to me, and the master who was too fond of the cane. He'd met this teacher, later in life and when the latter had approached him in a friendly way, he'd made it plain that he was not prepared to forgive and forget. He got great pleasure out of recounting the snub he had administered.

The other man was one of the few who discussed his post-war plans with me. Apparently he'd decided to go in for growing tomatoes by hydroponics, a technique he said was very new and of which I had never heard. I wonder if he carried out his plan and how successful it turned out to be.

But journeys come to an end, even long ones, and we arrived in Liverpool in a cold mid-December. We had travel warrants so there was no problem with booking the journey home that, in my case, was Birmingham. With my heavy, black kit-bag and knapsack (the term "rucksack" was hardly in use and "backpack" had not been invented) I hurried to the nearest post-office and sent a telegram home, announcing my arrival in England and the probable time my train would arrive in Birmingham.

All I can remember of the train journey is the effect of watching the small green fields, with their dark hedgerows slipping past. What a contrast to the vast stretches of brown earth, the water-logged paddy fields and the glaring lush vegetation to which I had become accustomed. This truly was "the green, green grass of home" and it engaged my feelings with a powerful tug.

Still wearing my bush-hat, with the bullet-sized, moth-eaten hole in it(!) I alighted at Birmingham Station. Lugging my kit-bag and with my pack on my back, I marched along the platform. To reach the exit one had to climb a flight of stairs and there, waiting at the top, was my wife, E. She kissed me, not very enthusiastically, and we went in search of a taxi. Once inside, I put my arm round her but little was said and we both felt somewhat constrained. I learnt later that she was put off by my bush-hat that seemed to signal that I had just come out of the jungle. Indeed, I learnt a lot in the coming days and weeks

The taxi deposited us at her home where her family were waiting to greet me and their demeanour, though hearty, increased the vague sense of unease that I had been experiencing since meeting E at the station. I remember that, despite the cold outside, the roaring coal fire in their small room made me feel like a roast chicken and, although I didn't know it at the time, this turned out to be an excellent metaphor of my situation.

During the evening, a number of E's friends arrived, no doubt for various reasons, to view the returning warrior. After they had gone she began to tell me about the many friends she had made at work, at the ice-skating rink, at the fencing club which she had joined and it dawned on me how, as a result of our enforced separation and the very different experiences we'd had, living, as it were, in different worlds, we had become estranged.

When my repatriation leave was over we were no closer in sympathy than when it started, indeed, things had worsened. I shall not go into the details of how and why our marriage rapidly deteriorated but will just record that, in the days, weeks and months that followed, I became increasingly depressed. This tortured state of mind lasted longer than it should have done because, after all my nostalgic longings when abroad, I was unwilling to take (with hindsight) the obvious step of cutting myself loose, physically and emotionally from what had become a hopeless relationship.

I was, of course, still in the army, and at the end of my leave had to report to the camp at Oulton Park just outside Chester. There I met Arthur again and we exchanged experiences. He also reported some domestic difficulties at first but, after his wife had had a good cry, they apparently settled down to married bliss. I was rather cautious in what I told him but he probably got some inkling of my predicament.

I soon became absorbed in the life of the camp and, as sergeant, had to undertake a number of responsibilities that kept my mind occupied. The post of editor for the camp news-sheet came up and, quoting my experiences with the forces journal I edited in India, *the BOR*, I applied and was appointed. Things went well, with congratulations on all sides on the first few issues. At one point, however, I came up against the CO's veto on some too "progressive" comment I made in an editorial.

It concerned the kind of life we should be expecting to lead on demobilisation and seemed to me fair comment. The CO thought otherwise and I had quite a row with the young pip-squeak who'd been detailed to keep an eye on me. I retained the editorial chair but the atmosphere had been soured and I was glad when the time came for my demobilisation.

Before this, however, I managed to obtain a place at the Army Formation College to do a course in English and History. The certificate I received at the end of this very interesting and quite testing course was evidence of perhaps the most advanced study I had yet undertaken and this was to stand me in good stead when I applied for a very different course, of which more later.

I do not remember the details of my demob notification but I can distinctly recall the almost dreamlike sensation of visiting the army store where they kept the stock of civilian clothing and choosing my first civvy suit. I can even remember that it was a kind of heather-and-fawn tweedy material and that I kept that suit for many a long year and wore it right through to the Fifties. I got little else of material value from the army, however, and this is not the place for a detailed evaluation of the effects of army life and experience on my character, intellect or understanding. To sum it up briefly, however: although, in the main, I disliked the army intensely for its mindless discipline and restrictions, amid these negative feelings, there were also some positive ones. It wasn't just the camaraderie, usually cited by the military as the great advantage of army life, although that was certainly a factor. There were also many very enjoyable episodes and real friendships and a meeting of minds

11

with many fellow conscripts. Neither can I leave the subject without remarking on the enlightening and emotional experiences I underwent in India, which have remained with me to the present day.

I returned from my first leave to live with E at her parents' home but, after a short further period of frustration and even despair, I felt able to make a decisive break, to move out and cut loose from an intolerable situation. Fortunately, my parents had now moved to Birmingham and I went to stay with them. I had, of course, been welcomed home by my parents and sisters and other relatives, who were naturally glad to see me again, safe and sound, after my long absence abroad.

I distinctly remember my heartache when I saw the tell-tale wrinkles round my mother's eyes, evidence of her anxiety for my safety and unhappiness at other things which had been happening whilst I was away. I learnt that she was not surprised at my decision to come and live with them. As there did not appear to be any immediate prospect of lucrative employment, I yielded to my father's urgings and started to work with him, as a temporary solution to the problem.

Those familiar with the first two volumes of my memoirs will know that he was in the so-called picture business. My task was to canvass from door to door and persuade people, usually women, to let me have a photograph of a loved-one so that my father's "firm" could enlarge it, without obligation and without charge as some sort of advertising ploy. This was followed by a visit from my father with the "unfinished proof" and the suggestion that they might like it "finished", or coloured and/or framed. My father, who used another firm to do all the technical work for him, had been in this one-man business all his working life.

I also resumed my Party political activity. The Party had a bookshop in Birmingham and this was the organising centre. There were two Welshmen in charge, the Birmingham full-time organiser Bert Williams and his assistant, Bert Pearce. The Cold War had already been initiated by Churchill's Fulton speech and the anti-Red hostility that this engendered was a considerable handicap to our political work.

On the other hand, the great promise of the first post-war Labour government, hailed with such enthusiasm by the whole Left, was beginning to crumble and we saw it as our duty to expose this retreat from the promises made, above all, to returning servicemen that "things would be very different" after the war. But our propaganda was never just negative.

We put forward alternative policies that often captured the popular mood and we gained considerable support. Unfortunately, the first-past-the-post election system meant that many who supported our policies, nonetheless voted for Labour and not for us "so as not to split the vote" and let the Tories in. Despite this, some of our comrades achieved sizeable votes, when we put up a hundred candidates in the first election after the war. Harry Pollitt, for instance, got around 4,500 when he stood in the Rhonda, pushing the Conservatives into third place and Willie Gallagher received well over 9,000 in West Fife, although he lost his seat and thus our parliamentary representation was wiped out. Calculating from the total votes our candidates received, I reckoned we had a voting support of some half-a-million in the country as a whole.

There were a number of popular Party leaders in Birmingham, at the time. Jessie Eden, a tough campaigning woman comrade, led the squatters' movement in which homeless people squatted in empty property. This was a national movement and in London my sister Trudy (as Gertie had renamed herself!) was involved, helping to occupy empty buildings with the best of them. This movement was so successful that when Ted Bramley, the Party Secretary in London, was taken to court for leading such an "illegal" activity, he was acquitted because he was able to establish that, as the judge put it, his motives were genuine concern for the homeless.

Another outstanding Party comrade in Birmingham was Professor George Thompson, who held the chair in Classics at the university and who was, for a time, on the Executive Committee of our Party. His pamphlet, *Marxism and Modern Poetry* , is still worth reading. There was also Rodney Hilton, one of his university colleagues in the History Department and several other academics. There was nothing surprising about this. Some of the most notable names in Academia nationally were also active members of the Party: Professor Haldane, the internationally known scientist; Professor Levy the mathematician; George Rudé, the British historian of the French Revolution and many others

This political activity and a number of other events began to revive my normal vivacity and love of life and to help me put the sad nature of my

13

return to England behind me. One of these was my contact with Birmingham Unity Theatre. I should explain (for those who have not read my last book, *Brighton Beach to Bengal Bay*) that London Unity Theatre had been formed in the Thirties by an amateur drama group I was in and several other similar groups who combined to construct their own theatre from an old chapel near Mornington Crescent.

They named it Unity Theatre and it became part of the great pre-war progressive, left-wing, anti-fascist, anti-war movement. It put on plays of "social significance", aimed to reach the highest artistic standards and, whilst having an educative, propagandist role, also wanted to bring the great works of drama to the "masses". Some leading professionals supported the theatre and Paul Robeson, the great black American actor/singer actually came and played in one of our productions. Provincial branches sprang up all over the country, in Manchester, Glasgow, Leeds etc. So I was delighted to find that there was one still going strong in Birmingham, after the war.

On my first attendance they were rehearsing a new J. B. Priestly play, *They Came to a City*. A group of diverse characters find themselves mysteriously transported to a spot outside the walls of a city. Each establishes their circumstances and viewpoints, the two main characters being Joe, the world-weary seaman who's "seen it all" and Alice, the downtrodden waitress with suppressed longings for a different sort of life.

Slowly the city gates open and they all go in. The second act sees them all returning and we learn about this strange city from their varied comments. It becomes clear that this is the socialist city of Priestley's imagination, although no detailed picture emerges of how it was organised. Alice and Joe, who have obviously become close, are both impressed with what they have seen. Alice wants to return before the gates shut forever but Joe says no, they have to go out and tell the world about it, that this is what they were "meant" to do. He persuades her that, together, they should do their bit, with millions of others, to try and change the world

The play finishes with a rousing call from Joe: "They'll tell you", he says, "that you can't change human nature. That's the oldest excuse in the world for doing nothing. And it isn't true; we've been changing human nature for thousands of years. But what you can't change.... is man's eternal desire... to make this world a better place to live in...."   Told in brief, the play

14

may sound purely propagandist but a reading of the whole would soon disabuse the reader of that idea.

Whilst the play was still in rehearsal and soon after I joined, the young man playing the lead left Birmingham and I was asked to step into his shoes. Nothing could have pleased me better. I grabbed the part with both hands and thoroughly enjoyed it, the more so because, within a few weeks, my leading lady (whom I shall call D) and I struck up a close relationship which lasted throughout the whole period of my stay in Birmingham.

D was also a member of The Clarion Singers, a workers' choir that performed traditional and progressive songs and had entertained people in air-raid shelters during the war. Alan Bush, the famous left-wing composer had also been associated with them at the time. It was led by Katherine Thomson, wife of Prof. Thomson, the classicist, and met and rehearsed in her house.

We staged *They Came to a City* in a very large hall, tickets being sold by our friends and acquaintances as well as by several of the local comrades. There was only one performance but the house was packed and the buzz in the atmosphere sent a thrill through the entire cast, waiting in the wings, with varying degrees of nervousness.

D and I really let ourselves go in the parts and this and the fine performance of the other players seemed to communicate itself to the audience who gave us a magnificent reception with repeated curtain calls. As we were about to retire to the dressing rooms to remove the grease-paint and change out of our costumes, I was surprised to see E standing before me.

Apparently she had been in the audience, and wanted to congratulate me on my performance, about which she was extremely enthusiastic. I gained the impression (confirmed some years later) that she deeply regretted our separation and wanted to return and let bygones be bygones. It was too late; the wounds had gone too deep. I thanked her for her kind words but refused to take the hint.

The next play, *This Trampled Earth*, was set in Spain at the time of the Franco dictatorship. I played the part of a fascist landowner who tries to seduce the fiancee of a local anti-fascist guerrilla leader, who is eventually shot down but the local people vow to fight on. I am told that I have a somewhat military bearing (a laugh really, considering my attitude to all things military!) and this seemed to suit the part, which I played with all the conviction I could muster, despite my loathing of the character. We put this play on in several venues and it was the last one in which I took part, as a very important turning point in my life had been reached which meant that I should have little time to devote to such leisure pursuits for some time to come.

Before this new stage in my life began, I went on holiday in Brighton with D. The weather was glorious and swimming in the sea again, my first opportunity since the war had ended, was sheer joy. Whilst there, I decided to visit my old school, Christ Church, in Bedford Place (The New Venture Theatre occupies the building today). I discovered that Mr.Russell, the former music teacher, was now Head and, to my amazement, he recognised me immediately. And he hadn't seen me since I was fourteen years old! I was delighted when he suggested that we should meet my old form teacher, for whom I had enormous respect, W. A. Gordon, known to all the boys as Wag.

We all dined together in a restaurant in East St. and Wag and I were full of reminiscences. I rather tactlessly told him he'd put on weight, which I think he mildly resented, but nothing could disturb our natural pleasure at meeting again. And when I told him of my plans, he remarked: "Well, you're a good actor and teaching is three parts acting. You'll do well!" Whether or not that confident prediction turned out to be accurate is a matter that could only be resolved by a detailed questioning of my past pupils: an unlikely undertaking!

TEACHING - AN OPPORTUNITY AND A CHALLENGE

As the war was coming to an end, we conscripts began to think about our future. Many, no doubt, had jobs to go back to. Some had been torn away from lucrative or absorbing careers, to which they were eager to return and which, in most cases, had been kept open for them. Some, however, were not at all keen to take up their old trades and professions or, even less, their humdrum jobs. Others, like myself, for instance, had not been trained for any work they considered worthwhile and had to think long and hard about what they were going to do, how they were going to earn a living.

Among its many promises to the population at large and to returning soldiers in particular, the Government put forward a scheme for training or retraining, which was to be made available to all servicemen and women, including those who had been conscripted into wartime work. One of the courses on offer was an Emergency Training Scheme for teachers. No previous academic qualifications were needed and entry to the scheme was to be by interview. If you could establish that, despite your lack of formal education, you were, nonetheless, "material" who could, with intensive training - one year was envisaged - be turned into a teacher, you were in.

I had a few minor certificates (RSA) and the one recently obtained at the Army Formation College, in English, Maths, History and Social Sciences, as well as a letter of recommendation from the colonel in charge of education at the Army Command in India and I had, indeed, engaged in a great deal of self-education, especially in history, partly arising out of my political activity. But my greatest strength was confidence and, to put it crudely, the gift of the gab. In short - I was accepted on the course.

The Birmingham Emergency Training College was situated in the Bristol Road, just a few hundred yards from the university. It was housed in prefabricated buildings but was really quite a comfortable place to inhabit. As my parents had just moved out of Birmingham and established themselves in a house in Golders Green in London, I became a boarder, as did most of the students, apart from those few who had homes locally.

This was my introduction to serious, post-school further education. I don't count the LCC evening classes that I attended in my early teens, which were undemanding and did not require much study out of lesson time. At

17

the training college we had to choose two special subjects to be studied more intensively. I chose History and English, the obvious choice considering my background and experience.

We were divided into tutor groups of about a dozen, with a personal tutor attached to each group, which met regularly. These group meetings were an important element in our training. They were both social and professional occasions at which we could bring up problems, air our views, consult with the tutor (which we could also do privately) and get to know each other more personally and individually.

The staff had been recruited from the various schools in and around the area and were usually practising teachers of long experience. The principal was Howard Cooksey, in many ways a remarkable man. He was tall, always dapper, with thinning grey hair smoothed round his scalp. He was not so much a tutor-lecturer-Head but, first and foremost - an entertainer. His addresses to the whole college were a joy to experience. One felt that the stage was his true profession. He would tell stories, act the buffoon, take himself down a peg or two - and we lapped it up.

Howard Cooksey, college principal.

His purpose, of course, was to put us in a good mood and he succeeded brilliantly. He knew he could leave the actual teaching to his very competent staff. The lecturer with whom I had most contact was a Miss Olive Lloyd. Tall, thin, middle-aged, grey hair slightly curled, she instantly became Olive Oyl to her disrespectful students. She had been a teacher in an Elementary (later Secondary Modern) School and taught us History and Education.

The intellectual snobs in the class, amongst whom I half include myself, were rather derisory about her grasp of grammar and general linguistic competence but she knew her stuff, especially in teaching technique. I shall never forget one perceptive illustrative example she gave us. "Be yourself and don't attempt to copy someone else's methods, they may not suit you," she told us. "Just imagine me trying to put on the performance that the principal does!" The thought of her acting the clown, which he did so successfully, was enough to underline the point she was making.

My fellow-students came from a wide variety of backgrounds, the only common feature being their wartime membership of the armed forces or having been conscripted to some other war-related work. Some had been officers, others only of lowly rank; some had been academics; others were Secondary School educated but most, I imagine, like myself, had very little in the way of academic education. There were some fine sportsmen amongst them, some ex-journalists, office workers, salesmen (like me!) and a few - I don't think many - had been manual workers.

I soon struck up friendships with a number of them. There was Larry Green, with whom I am still in touch and who later became a long-standing member of the NUT executive committee. Jim Murphy, another of my close associates was also to reach the heights in the Union, achieving the honoured position of national president one year. Larry lived locally and invited me to his home where I met his attractive wife, Leonore (Len to her friends). Len was most friendly and welcoming and I spent many a happy hour with them and sometimes stayed the weekend. Our political outlook was similar and this helped to cement the friendship, although I had many friends of quite different political persuasion.

Larry Green (above) and me.

Among the staff, apart from the principal and Miss Lloyd, the lecturer I felt most kinship with was Mr.Evernden, the English tutor. He had a wonderfully free and easy style and usually began with an anecdote connected with some recent experience. He would begin: "I saw this chap gazing into a shop window..." and then go on to build up to character analysis, effect of appearance, and so on.

He was keen on poetry and introduced us to a number of poems and poets that were new to me. A particular favourite of his was Gerald Manley Hopkins. I still have the copy he gave us of *Brinsley Poplars Felled* and can recall from memory the first few lines:

> *My poplars dear,*
> *Whose airy cages quelled,*
> *Quelled and quenched*
> *The living sun;*
> *All gone.*

I think I can say that he saw me as one of the outstanding members of the English group and asked me to write the editorial of the college magazine. He was also an enthusiastic drama teacher. There was an experienced actor and producer in the group, Jack Beckett, and we immediately went into rehearsal for a morality play, *Youth,* which Jack produced as well as playing the name part. I played opposite him as the moralist, lecturing him (and the audience) about his profligacy and youthful abandon. A sexy female student played the role of Lechery, with great conviction! We also did *The Man Born to be King*, by Dorothy L. Sayers and, yes, you've guessed it, I played the role of Christ wearing, oddly enough, the same costume that I'd worn in the previous play.

In addition to professionally written drama, we also wrote and produced our own little sketches for the classroom, and I shall never forget the scene in which I played a mutineer on board ship and had an altercation with the captain, played by a very humorous type. As we squared up to each other, eyeball to eyeball, we were never able to complete the scene without collapsing into helpless laughter. Another entertainment that we put on for the whole college, was written by a team of us, each writing one scene, largely about college life. This went down very well and apparently the principal was observed rocking with mirth in his seat.

The students formed a number of clubs and I was active in several of them. Part of the reference given to me by my personal tutor at the end of the course, reads as follows:

"In the community life of the college Mr. Goldman ....has served as an elected member of the   Students' Council, Chairman of the Dramatic Society, Chairman of the Social Studies   Committee......and was a member of the Committee of the Political Society."

Politics, as the reader will have realised by now, came as second nature to me and it wasn't long before most people knew where I stood. This made me some friends but also many enemies especially, and to my disadvantage, among the tutors.

My tutor had slightly underestimated my position in the Political Society as I actually became its secretary. In this position I organised many meetings with outside speakers. One series of meetings invited, on different nights, a speaker from each of the three main political parties and also one from the Communist Party. I can distinctly remember that, at the meeting addressed by the Conservative representative, I made an impassioned denunciation of the sufferings caused by the slump in the Thirties and the heartless attitude of the then Conservative government. I don't know how the rest of the meeting responded but the speaker applauded, perhaps satirically.

We also organised a mock election. I've forgotten who the Tory was but I know that the Liberal was a small, blonde, excitable Welshman. A very nice, personable chap was the Labour Party candidate and I represented the Party. The campaign was fierce but great fun, with notices and posters up all over the college, some serious, some humorous. I put up a notice quoting the Dean of Canterbury, to the effect that real Christianity, as preached by the Founder himself, was only practised in the Soviet Union, where no-one was allowed to profit from another man's labour. That put the cat among the pigeons, I can tell you!

We held election meetings, of course, and I gave out some Party leaflets at mine. At question time, one student who had read our leaflet on the railways, challenged some of the statistics in what he called, "this Russian leaflet". I pretended not to understand his reference to the Russians but as the figures given were from government publications, I was able to assure him that the sources were English - and official. He probably didn't believe me but would certainly not take the trouble to check.

There was little rancour, however, in the campaign as there was a great deal of genuine camaraderie in the student body. The result of the election was a tie between Liberal and Labour. I got 30 votes (out of 200-odd) and the Tory not much more. I was gratified when the Labour candidate told me, in confidence, that he'd voted for me and I had no reason to disbelieve him. The run-off resulted in a Liberal victory.

During the year, we had three stints of teaching practice. The first was in a Junior School and the other two in Secondary Moderns, the new name for Elementary Schools!. Emergency trained teachers were obviously not to be trusted to teach Grammar School pupils. Although I was one of those being trained for teaching in Secondary education, it was considered good policy to let us experience the lower age groups, if only for a few weeks of practice. I found it very refreshing, making contact with the under-elevens.

My last practice was extremely rewarding. The Head of the school had a custom of asking the trainee, if he were an English specialist, to rehearse and produce a group for choral speaking. As drama (both acting and producing) was a speciality of mine, I relished the opportunity. I've forgotten what the piece was that we did but it received a great ovation when the group performed it at a school assembly.

I also remember that school because the Head was so sympathetic and helpful. He was also, I suspected from conversations I had with him, on the Left politically and, as can be imagined, this endeared him to me especially. The class teacher with whom I worked closely at the school was a very helpful character, too. On my last day, he told me the class wished to give me a present and I asked for a copy of Joyce's *Portrait of the Artist as a Young Dog*. He brought this along to the college, signed by every member of the class and including very nice dedicatory comments, and he handed it to the principal as I wasn't available. The latter was suitably impressed.

This episode was particularly important because it came at a time when a small group of tutors was trying to persuade the principal that I was a subversive influence who should not be let loose on the children. They cited one of my lesson notes for a lesson I had prepared to use with a radio programme. The subject was the colonisation of America and its effects on the native population. I had thought that my approach was pretty innocuous

22

but it obviously gave these people the opportunity they had been seeking for some time to "put the boot in". They also referred to various other supposed misdemeanours of mine, already dealt with by the principal.

To do him credit, he resisted their attempt to blacken my name but, as a sop to their *amour propre*, he agreed to send an inspector in to the school to observe my lessons. This was normally done when a student was either seen to be failing or else was noted as exceptionally good. In my case, it was the former. However, the Head told me that, when the inspector arrived, he met him with the remark that he had been expecting an inspection because I was "the best student he had ever had". Even in my most conceited moments, I realise that this was pure hyperbole but I'm sure he felt he was helping me in my career. It certainly put my opponents' noses out of joint.

When I was duly awarded my teaching certificate, I applied for and obtained a post in London, where I could live with my parents. I said goodbye to D with no definite decision made about our future. I was, in any case, still technically married (divorce came considerably later). She had also started on a teacher training course, inspired, perhaps, by what I had told her about mine. We maintained contact by letter and an occasional visit to a mutually suitable trysting place. But inevitably, I suppose, as I was certainly not inclined to seek marriage again, our relationship petered out - and she married a fellow-student.

By the time I had completed my college course, my parents had already moved to London and taken up residence in Hillcrest Avenue, Temple Fortune, not far from Golders Green. There was ample room for me to stay there so, as I had no further interest in remaining in Birmingham, I decided to start my new career in the capital. After a short period in Amberley Secondary Modern School in Paddington, I was transferred by the Authority to Acland School in Kentish Town. I wrote and told the Deputy Head at Amberley and he sent me an encouraging reply. He "wasn't best pleased" at the news as he seems to have been impressed with what he saw of my teaching in the one term I was there. He thought I had made a wise decision to take up teaching and, "I should be surprised if you do not make your mark."

Acland was a Central School, something of an anomaly in the tri-partite system set up by the 1944 Education Act. Its was an all-boys school for those who had "just failed" the Eleven-plus (of which more, much

23

more, later!). Consequently, its curriculum aped that of the Grammar School and it trained some pupils for the GCE "O" Level Examination. I was engaged to teach English and History.

The Head Teacher was Freddy Pearson, a blubbery sack of a man, whose medium height only emphasised his flabby bulk. He had a country accent of some sort, was red of face and watery of eye, wore an untidy baggy grey suit and had an unpleasant habit of grabbing you by the arm when he addressed you. He was pleasant enough in the early days and even complimented me with: "You interviewed well" after I had been taken on.

His attitude to the boys seemed to me unhealthy, especially as he didn't shrink from criticising his staff sometimes in front of the pupils, when he ought to have been backing up their disciplinary methods. For instance, he laid down strict rules about setting homework, especially for the examination boys, but when I once referred some to him because they hadn't done their homework, he told them to take no notice. He actually told me this, himself, when I raised the matter with him some time later!

To begin with, my closest colleague was Lawrence Snell, a bearded, red-haired Cornishman, resembling the portraits one sees of Francis Drake, only much taller and beefier than Drake is usually portrayed. Lawrence was a historian of some standing but as, for some reason, the Head wanted to reward him with a higher post, he was made Head of English. He had dropped out of his Divinity course at Oxford because, half-way through it, he had converted to Roman Catholicism. He had, however, been made an Associate of the Royal Historical Society on the basis of a study he made (and published) about the Reformation in Cornwall and also a history of the Duke of Cornwall's Light Infantry. He had a slight stutter when excited and was meticulous in all his habits. He had a lively mind, made incendiary statements of the "shoot-the-lot" variety, especially about Reds, but with a twinkle in his eye, when arguing with me that, unsurprisingly, happened quite a lot.

He once invited me home to sample his wife's heavenly Cornish pasties. At the end of the very satisfying meal, he turned to me, rather unexpectedly and said: "Right, now explain to me what this communism of yours is all about!" I'm afraid he wasn't very impressed with my explanation. "Most people are very content with the way things are", he said, "Why do you people have to go around stirring things up?" There was no short answer to that and we had to agree to differ. Despite this, we became friends and still, over 50 years later, exchange Christmas cards.

Then there was Byron Munday, an ex-RAF Welshman who, having been shot down over the coast of Europe, had been a prisoner-of-war and apparently returned to England almost a living skeleton. Not that you could have imagined it looking at him in 1948. Quite the contrary; although he was slim he was very fit and was, in fact, the PE teacher and, from what I could see, a pretty good footballer. He was also very practical and did quite a lot of interior decorating on the side.

One winter, just before Christmas, he was away sick with a bad cold. By this time we had established a certain friendly relationship and I decided it might be a nice gesture if I called round with a small gift of some sort for the family. So, I bought a chicken and took it round. That was when I met the family for the first time. There was Connie, his charming and welcoming wife and his two gorgeous little daughters, Margaret (Maggie) and Barbara (Babs or Sukie). I was greatly attracted to this family atmosphere and they seemed to welcome me in. From that time onwards, I became a regular visitor. I don't know if they adopted me or I adopted them but I looked upon Maggie and Babs as my surrogate daughters. I remember taking them to a pantomime and they treated me like a favoured uncle.

This friendship with "By" and his family greatly enriched my life at that time, when I was feeling unattached and restless. It gave me an anchor, somewhere, other than my own home, where I could feel comfortable, at ease and among friends. Each Christmas, I walked across the Heath from my house to theirs, taking presents and greetings. Believe it or not, I still have the shoe-cleaning set the girls gave me for Christmas 1957!

Another colleague who became a firm friend was Roy Fitchett, a young artist who took over the Art department from an older man who retired soon after I arrived. Roy's whole approach was so drastically different from that of his predecessor that the results were immediately noticeable. Where the other man was formal and pedantic to an exaggerated degree - he started all beginners by getting them to draw each letter of the alphabet! - Roy believed in free expression; his guiding hand was there but quite imperceptible.

The walls of many classrooms were soon decorated with the pupils' artwork, some of it startlingly good. I was particularly impressed with his influence on one of the very disruptive boys in my own class. Roy discovered this boy's artistic abilities, encouraged and developed them, giving the boy a self-esteem he had hitherto lacked. Both the boy and I profited from the transformation this made in his whole attitude. The boy's efforts were crowned with glory when one of the school governors, seeing a painting of his in the Head's study, asked if she could buy it and take it home!

There was an elderly colleague in the English department, Charles Green, who deserves special mention and who also became a close friend. Although nearing the end of his career he was anything but stiff and formal in his approach and his attitude to the boys was similar to mine. That is to say he was not heavily judgmental, assumed every pupil had creative ability and was prepared to give them their head. Though he sometimes carried this to anarchical extremes, I recognised that he had a genuine concern for their humanity.

At first we clashed politically, especially in the union (NUT) where we were both regular attendants, until we gradually reached an understanding and found that even ideologically we had much in common. There were many other interesting characters on the staff but space prevents my going into too much detail. Bob, another PE man, was a great, strong, athletic type who had also been a prisoner-of-war but had fared far better than By. He was a simple fellow, the eternal schoolboy, full of practical jokes and inclined to be a bit of a bully and very right-wing in his views. Surprisingly, we got on quite well and occasionally had a night out together - two bachelors on the prowl.

Now that my new career was under way, I set about what I regard as the main tasks in education: getting to know the pupils, preparing and delivering my lessons and, most important of all, helping in the fullest development of young human beings. Apart from acting as a form master, I first of all had the "O" Level class for History and later, when Mr. Snell wanted to take over History, I was given the English examination class. So, in each case, I studied the syllabus laid-down by the authority as well as looking up as many past papers as I could get hold of.

This was my first long-term encounter with the adolescent and pre-adolescent male. They came in all shapes and sizes and, more importantly, in all sorts of moods, from the interested and friendly down to the truculent and surly. And I was to be their mentor, to pass on information and skills and encourage them to develop enquiring minds that would lead them to seek out ideas and data for themselves and then go on to be model(!) citizens.

My idea was that the result should not only enable them to pursue a career and make a living and even get work satisfaction, but also to become rounded individuals who could enjoy life to the full and take their place in society, able to cope with the realities of life and even change those realities if they were dissatisfied with them. A tall order? Indeed it was and I wonder to what extent, if at all, I ever achieved that high ambition.

The history I taught them started with pre-history. I loved to dwell on the dinosaurs and I think they did too. A visit to the Natural History Museum was built in to the first-year course. That huge diplodocus that greeted you in the hall in those days, remains imprinted on my memory and it certainly fired our imagination. The differentiation of humans from the rest of the animals was also a favourite theme of mine, listing all the advantages that made homo sapiens the dominant creature on the planet.

In English, I adopted the "creative" approach, although the "O" level syllabus demanded an understanding of complex sentences. I had to learn this first, myself, and discovered that I had been speaking in complex sentences all my life without realising it! But it was the creative side that I enjoyed and wanted them to enjoy as well. Mr. Evernden had given us some stimulating ideas and one I tried, with some success, was called "viewpoint".

The purpose was to force the pupils to observe minutely simple actions and record only what they saw. "He did this or that" was out. "I saw" was in. Watching someone putting their hand in their pocket meant the gradual disappearance of the finger tips, then the fingers, then the palm and so on. Even some of the dullest boys produced quite vivid descriptions in this way. Another activity we had learnt at college was mime. I started a first-year mime group, which met after school as well and put on performances for the whole school. When news of its success got out, the group began to take part in drama festivals at St. Pancras Town Hall. Mr. Green, who took an intense interest in this activity and gave me every encouragement, produced the programme for this event and included some witty comments about each mime.

On Parade! The smallest boy is the sergeant, drilling his squad.
His mouth is wide open but not a word emerges.

It is well known that older pupils, especially boys, are rather inhibited when it comes to public performances, particularly of such a "silly" thing as mime. But I noted with pleasure that, once I had started them in the first year, they continued to perform and enjoy it right through the school, even when they reached adolescence. It is a sufficient commentary on the man and his outlook that Mr. Pearson didn't really approve. He didn't consider it "real drama". But fortunately I only discovered this much later on.

There was a good deal of emphasis on sport and I helped to run a table-tennis club. On one occasion a boy slyly introduced a sponge-covered bat with which he was able to achieve his long-held ambition to turn the tables (literally) on me and hand me a humiliating defeat! There was also one sports day in which my voice was again in demand as announcer and general oral organiser.

But the activity which I remember with the greatest satisfaction and which, I think, both gave me pleasure and, at the same time, enabled me to fulfil one of the educational aims I mentioned at the start, was youth-hostelling. I had long been a member of the YHA from my youth in the Thirties. I now took out Life membership and persuaded a number of the pupils to join, too.

I felt that these London inner-city youngsters were thoroughly deprived of the freshness of country air and of the insight into other environments and ways of living.

Such trips not only provided them with healthy exercise, they also broadened their horizons and introduced them to forms of enjoyment they had never encountered or even considered before. That, even at their tender age, they and their parents realised this, is borne out by the many letters of appreciation I received both at the time and later, when I was leaving the school. Byron and his family frequently accompanied us on these outings, which were usually over a whole weekend. What a grand social and socialising experience they turned out to be.

YHA group, including Byron, Connie and their children.

I was now fully launched in my new career, a career I had never dreamed I should be able to follow. The semi-educated schoolboy who became a salesman, with no serious training and only his native wits to guide him had, himself, become an educator. All the experiences of commerce, the army, India, political engagement, brought together and metamorphosed into some sort of a briefly trained professional, over a period of some eleven months, had flung me, head first, into the maelstrom of the classroom. And - I had at least survived, even survived with some honour, though not a few metaphorical bruises.

EDUCATION - THE GREAT DEBATE BEGINS

As soon as I began my training I had joined the NUT, the main teachers' union and now that I was working I started attending the monthly meetings of their St. Pancras Association. This branch was dominated by members from local Roman Catholic schools and I soon learnt that the committee was chosen by a system in which the word went round to these schools who to vote for and, equally important, who not to vote for! It seems that the union was a battleground between members of differing outlooks and, especially, political leanings.

So the committee was largely composed of staid right-wing types who didn't want anybody to rock the boat. They wanted a quiet life, were "palsy-walsy" with the authority and opposed to change of any kind. Any talk of militant action was taboo. They couldn't stop it at association meetings but they could see to it that that was as far as it got. What might be called "the opposition" consisted of assorted left-wing types, either from the Party or the Labour Party, among the latter of whom I had a number of friends. The main points of contention were salaries and educational policy.

The Right were organised in the surreptitious way I have indicated. I didn't know if they got together in formal meetings in which they schemed to "keep the Reds out" or whether it was all done privately in people's homes - or maybe in the church hall! The Labour Party colleagues were members of the National Association of Labour Teachers and I and other comrades formed groups throughout London (and the country as a whole) of Communist Party teachers. We held open public meetings attended by a widely varied audience, mainly of the Left, of course, but not solely. My friend Charles Green, for instance, came along to several meetings and, be it said, made many a sensible comment - and criticism.

It should be made clear that the Party leadership did not dictate to us what our educational policy should be. Rather it was the other way round and we were officially "educational advisers" to the EC. The Conservative Party, by the way, also had its organisation within the teaching profession, as did the Trotskyites. It was about this time that the whole question of educational organisation of state schools arrived on the agenda. The 1944 Act had been a great leap forward, abolishing Elementary Schools and making all 11+

education "Secondary". But that was where the contentious problem began. There were to be three different types of Secondary education to match the perceived three different "types" of child!

It soon became evident that this division simply continued the old divided and divisive system. Now it was the Grammar Secondaries that were to take the "intelligent" (read middle class) children, about 20% of the total, and the rest were to be allocated to the Secondary Moderns ie the old Elementaries with a new name. The former were to prepare pupils for the GCE "O" Level, the entry to the gateway to Higher Education. Pupils in the latter were not considered "capable of benefiting from an academic education." There was a third choice (hence the expression "tri-partite" education); these were the Secondary Technical Schools that took pupils at 13. There were very few of these and they impinged little on the educational debate

It was not only our Party which challenged the whole concept behind this selective system. Large numbers of educationists, both academic and practical, and many politicians from Liberals leftwards (and even including some progressive Tories) could see the terrible damage that this divisive system was inflicting on the nation's youth. It should be noted that the Labour Party top brass was wedded to the system because "it gave the clever working-class child a chance to rise."

The whole system was underpinned by the so-called Intelligence Test, purporting to establish a child's Intelligence Quotient. And the battle raged around this game of picking the winners, ie trying to forecast a child's whole future intellectual development. The old, old question of nature versus nurture. Some thought the method of selection flawed and there were many attempts to refine the tests. We went much further. We condemned the whole supposed separation of the sheep from the goats. Human beings are neither sheep nor goats and their future development is impossible to predict. Indeed, the attempt itself has a bearing on a child's performance, giving extra confidence (sometimes misplaced) to those picked and destroying it in those rejected. And we teachers had to pick up the pieces.

Genetic inheritance no doubt plays its part in a person's abilities. But *what* part? How much influence has the family background, poverty, bad housing, parental attitudes and abilities and so on? And, most vital of all, how much corrective influence can the educational system have? Telling a child that it "can't" is hardly an encouragement or motivating force. And motivation is the key to achievement in all fields of activity.

All these arguments and counter arguments were raging just as I began my teaching career and I jumped into the fray, buoyed up and spurred on by the brilliant work of comrades like Professor Brian Simon, whose books on Intelligence Testing are seminal works, and Max Morris, Head of a Grammar School (!) and later to become President of the NUT. Even as far back as that, things were changing and the old attitude that "some are born dull and there's not much you can do about it" was being challenged, not merely in theoretical argument but in practice. In many Secondary Modern Schools teachers, defying the prevailing culture, were training these "failures" to sit - and pass - the "Grammar School exam" ie the GCE (O Level).

I began to meet many like-minded teachers, teaching in north-west London, some in the Party, some members of the National Association of Labour Teachers and many others, unattached to any particular party or ideological persuasion but simply interested in genuine education for all. Among the highly capable and enthusiastic Party comrades in the profession, in our area, the most outstanding was Ian Gunn. Ian was a physical giant of a man whose intellect matched his physique. He had all the facts and figures at his finger-tips, had read the relevant material as it was published, knew the ins and outs of the system and was highly regarded and respected even by those who profoundly disagreed with his views. He edited the Party's educational journal, *Education Today and Tomorrow,* which I and other comrades sold to colleagues in our own schools. The publication contained articles on every aspect of the school system and teachers' pay and conditions, and played its part in the movement for Comprehensive Schools, the logical demand for those who wanted to see the end of selection and the hated Eleven-plus. The ETT gave rise to many a fruitful discussion with colleagues to whom I had sold it and who wanted to challenge some of its contents. I became its reviewer of the latest educational literature and followed up my reviews with requests for advertisements from the publishers.

There was quite a group of progressive teachers with whom I established friendships. John Dixon, a Northumbrian intellectual, was perhaps the most outstanding of these. A member of NALT and a Labour Party

32

activist, he championed the so-called child-centred method of education. He was opposed to strict - and restricting - rules and regulations and believed in giving the pupils their head, with plenty of stimulating encouragement but without neglecting the need for clarity. Rules were only valuable, he held, because they worked if you wanted to get your thoughts and feelings across to others. The desire to do so, however, must come first.

But the teacher had to demonstrate that the rules worked or the pupil would not accept them. So it was not sloppy, abrogation of responsibility by the teacher, which was the usual accusation against this approach. John and I became firm friends and I noted that he was proud of his Northumbrian accent, rather like D. H. Lawrence and his Nottingham mode of speech. I was frequently invited to his large flat not far from Belsize Park where his wife, Molly, also a Northumbrian, served me with her delicious scones. She taught Classics in a Grammar School.

John's great pal was Sid Lubin, who went even further than John did in his ideas of freedom in the classroom but, although I did occasionally raise an eyebrow at what I saw there, the pupils seemed to understand what was expected of them and produced some excellent work. Sid lived with an aunt who had brought him up. I visited him often and soon got used to the chaotic state of his room. He was an ardent collector of records, mainly classical, and his room was littered with them from floor to ceiling. Taking tea with him meant searching for some safe spot to put your cup!

There was a remarkable coincidence about another colleague and comrade who taught in the area. His name was Sid Lytton and we first met in Calcutta where we were both stationed during the war and he and I were part of the circle of British and American servicemen who congregated at the home of a wonderfully friendly and warm hearted Bengali family, the Sircars, whom I describe in some detail in my previous book, *Brighton Beach to Bengal Bay.*

The debate about how to help the young develop their abilities is no academic exercise. It has deep implications for the whole of our society. Stifle a person's talents and their stunted personality can lead to great social harm. Encourage and further their personal development and we will all be repaid a thousandfold. Education does not mean being stuffed with facts; it means having a generous and enquiring mind, interested in every aspect of life and nature and always hungry to find out more. This will never be achieved by looking for sheep and goats and dancing on a pinpoint to ascertain the differences. A class is a community, part of the wider community of the school and life outside. All that brings this community together, helps it to advance together must be persistently encouraged. That's education - and that's what I was aiming at in my new, inspiring profession.

PERSONAL DEVELOPMENT

A host of other names and faces and personalities crowd into my vision, for whom there is no space here, so I come to the next considerable step in my career, namely, the opportunity to study at university. One of the conditions attached to the emergency training was that when it was completed and the certificated teachers started in their profession, they were obliged to take up a course of acceptable study, in their spare time, for another two years at least, which would be free of charge.

We were told that no intense, high-level study was envisaged, just "something to satisfy the authorities," perhaps, if you were in London, LCC evening classes in any subject of your choice and not necessarily aiming at any particular examination. However, I approached it from the opposite angle: not, "what can I get away with that is not too intellectually demanding?" but "what is the highest level of study I can get them to pay for?"

I decided that this was my only - certainly my first and probably my last – opportunity for serious Higher Education. In short, nothing would satisfy me but to study for a degree. I should have liked to do a History degree but understood that this would entail an entrance exam including Latin. I hadn't the stomach for this so plumped for an Economics degree at the London School of Economics where no such regulation existed. But the question was: would the authorities wear it? The cost of university study is far higher than they had bargained for and the course would take five years!

I was called before yet another interviewing committee, the chairman of which, as luck would have it, was H.L.Beales, chairman of a local Grammar School near Acland and also, incidentally, editor of Penguin Books and, most important of all, on the teaching staff at LSE. I must confess that I enjoyed the interview thoroughly and I think the panel realised that they were not dealing with some callow youth but someone whose experience of life (if not of learning) was as great as theirs and in some cases greater, as my whole pre-war and war-time experience was reviewed.

Towards the end, Beales, who had been very helpful throughout, smiled a little smile and said: "Well, it seems to me we've already largely agreed to let Mr. Goldman in," thus brooking no contradiction, and he assured me that they all wished me success in my studies. And that was that. It only remained for me to persuade the LCC to pay the fees which, after much "argy-bargying", they agreed to do.

I'm not sure that I really knew what I'd let myself in for but it was clearly a mammoth undertaking. At 32, having little or no experience of serious academic study and only just starting a career in what was to prove a very stressful occupation, I was to begin a five-year evening course, requiring regular attendance at lectures, library research, note-taking, essay-writing and acres of print to read. And, being footloose and fancy free, I wanted some social life, too!

My fellow-students were from a variety of backgrounds. As far as I knew, none of them were teachers. Most had undergone a more advanced education than I, some were ex-Public-School, some from various financial institutions, studying economics in the country's most prestigious institution for that subject and wishing to further their careers; some were foreign. One young man was the son of Jewish refugees from Germany, who told me: "I'm a sowshalist." There were, indeed, quite a bevy of left-wing students at LSE at that time. Small wonder, when you consider that one of the best-known lecturers on Politics was Harold Laski, a member of the triumvirate that headed the Left Book Club.

There were Right-wingers there, too, however and many and furious were the clashes in the students' union and other debating platforms. I tried to maintain a constant attendance at lectures and seminars but this was not always possible and I sometimes chose the primrose path of dalliance and neglected my studies. But, on the whole, I was a diligent student, my main problem being the division of my energies between my professional duties and my studies.

The Economics lectures, always theoretical of course, became increasingly mathematical and complex and not terribly interesting because, as someone with extensive experience of real life, I found the models presented to us difficult to reconcile with reality and also because I came to the subject with already formed ideas which clashed with some of the theories being put forward.

Laski's lectures on Politics were certainly interesting, but I was highly critical even of these. I was always testing the ideas against my own experience and often found them sadly wanting. One of the most fascinating lectures I attended was by Sir Arnold Plant, who had been a government adviser during the war. His subject was the economics of availability. A top hat or evening dress might be seldom used but it was - available. And that was an economic value in itself. But my main subject was Economic History, the chief lecturer in which was Walter Stern, and within this I concentrated on the period of the Industrial Revolution. Despite this specialisation, I am forced to admit that my best grade in the final examination (a One, in fact) was for the compulsory essay, which had nothing at all to do with any of the subjects studied and was entitled: *Evidence for the existence of ghosts.*

My participation in the social life of the School was strictly limited, for obvious reasons, and though I made a number of contacts, both political and social, I did not retain them when the course was finished. That moment arrived at the end of the summer term in 1953, when, at the advanced age of 37, I was able to add the title letters BSc (Econ) to my name, after a ceremony at the Albert Hall, for which I hired an academic gown and mortar-board (never seen or worn again) to accept my degree from the Chancellor of London University, who just happened to be - the Queen Mother!

Before leaving the subject of my brush with academe, perhaps I should mention an opportunity that came my way to take part in an archaeological "dig" in Cornwall. Apparently they had uncovered a Saxon village there and wanted eager hands and arms to help with the digging. It sounded like fun, if hard work, so I attached myself to the party and found the whole thing both exhilarating and intensely interesting. And when an actual coin was unearthed, we felt all our efforts had been worthwhile. Whilst I was digging, but unbeknown to me, the leader of the dig took a series of photographs of me in action, with the long, Cornish spades with which they had fitted us out. I must admit, in all modesty, that it looked quite impressive. He said he would exhibit the snaps for the others to see "how it should be done". I can't recall whether he carried out this "threat".

Archaeological "dig". I'm leaning on the shovel.

Back at the school chalk-face, the ongoing educational debate and the campaign we were waging for Comprehensive Schools meant that I wanted to teach in one of these, myself. The LCC had started to introduce a few experimental Comprehensives: Holloway Grammar School, around the corner from Acland, was one of these. So when I saw a vacancy there in the History department, I immediately applied.

I already knew at least two members of the staff there. One was George Rudé, Head of History, a highly academically qualified teacher, unable to obtain a university post because of his politics. I met George, who later became a firm friend, for a short chat, to test out the water, so to speak though, of course, he had no say in the appointment. The other colleague was John Dixon, referred to above. Another very progressive colleague there was Louis Watt, brother of Watson Watt, of nuclear physics fame.

The Head and Deputy were good, academically well qualified Grammar School types, who had no doubt held their positions before the Comprehensive transformation. There didn't seem much chance of real comprehensive thinking there. Most of the other colleagues were of similar stamp, with similar educational standpoints. The school was thoroughly streamed and had a reputable sixth form, many of whose members regularly obtained places at university.

I was now faced with a much wider variety of pupils, both socially and intellectually. There were a number of ex-Grammar School boys, largely from middle-class or professional homes. A few had well known parents. There were the Swingler boys. Their father was a Labour MP and their uncle, Randall, who had returned from the war a broken man who died soon after, had been a regular contributor to the Daily Worker and a poet of some distinction. A friend of theirs was David Vorhaus, whose father, Bernard, was American, a film producer whose death last year merited a half-page obituary in the Guardian. He had migrated to Britain along with a number of other left-wing Americans, as a refugee from McCarthyite terror. I became a regular visitor to their home.

The presence of such pupils and the contact one had with their parents certainly enlivened the whole atmosphere and added to the general ferment of ideas which, as I have indicated previously, was swirling around in educational circles and into which I frequently added my two-pennyworth.

All was not sweetness and light, however. There were also the usual proportion of difficult and disruptive pupils and though some of these were by no means dullards (some, indeed, were a little too "bright"!) there were also a fair number of pupils of low attainment. And all these had to be dealt with and encouraged to develop.

I decided to continue the practice I had started at Acland and invite any interested pupils to accompany me on YHA weekends. I remember several boys, whose names I have unfortunately forgotten, whose personal development was clearly influenced by these outings. The main point was that the constraints of school life could be abandoned and, in that freer atmosphere, we could get to know each other and understand and even sympathise with each other's foibles. They took to calling me by my first name on these rambles but always switched back to normal practice when we returned to school on Monday. John Dixon and some of his class occasionally accompanied us on these trips.

My social life also had to be attended to and as soon as I returned to London, I again made contact with friends and relatives, many of whom I'd seen little - or not at all - since I returned from the army. There were my sisters, Helen, married to Reuben and living in Barnet, and Trudy, still unmarried and, like me, living with our parents. It was a big, three-storeyed house and Etta and her husband, Jack, also came to live there. During this period, Etta became pregnant but moved out before her gorgeous little daughter, Jennifer, was born: my parents' first grandchild!

My parents in the 1950's

39

Our neighbours were a delightful family, the Gauntletts. Mrs. G was a widow, with two adult children, Bernard, a balance-control engineer at the BBC - he had "perfect pitch" - and Pam, a gifted pianist and music teacher. Bernard and I struck up a friendship that lasted until his tragic death from Parkinson's disease. He joined the Party soon after I got to know him and this, of course, cemented our friendship. But his father (an officer in the army in India, I believe) would have been horrified and I don't suppose his sister and mother were too keen, either.

Our family were a boisterous lot, with plenty of altercation between the generations and we must have disturbed the neighbours quite a bit. But Mrs. G, a true Christian, never uttered a word of complaint and, indeed, was very friendly and helpful. Pam, who later married a lovely German chap, an amateur violinist, who died, a few years ago of a heart complaint, is the only one remaining and we are still in touch with her and visit each other from time to time.

Whilst still living in Birmingham, I had travelled to London and made contact again with my old friend, Wolfie, who had re-styled himself, Wulf. He was now married to Lulu, daughter of a distinguished Russian Jewish family, of intellectual bent. Though her father was in business, in the wool trade, all six children (two boys and four girls) had embraced academe and it was at Cambridge that Wulf and Lulu had met. When I first visited them in the family home in a beautiful house in Hampstead, they already had one little son, Nicky and he was soon followed by the birth of a daughter, Judy.

Wulf had a position in the Civil Service, in which he had been engaged during the war, on vital war work and had thus not been conscripted into the Forces, so that our experiences had been vastly different. But it was a great pleasure to meet up with him again and to be accepted into the family, including his new one and as soon as I moved to London I became a frequent visitor there, sometimes staying the night.

I also got in touch with my old friend, Abe Games, who had become a well known poster artist before the war and had followed this up by working for the government during the war, producing some very remarkable posters on a variety of subjects. Abe treated me to a slap-up dinner at the Marble Arch Corner House. During the meal he expanded on his favourite topic: the artist in all of us, pointing to how my tie matched my shirt and both went well with my suit. But he also had views, usually eccentric ones, on almost every other subject. It led to a fascinating exchange, as I'm not all that backward when it comes to responding to other people's views. Abe died a few years ago and got very extensive obits. in the Guardian and elsewhere.

I visited my cousin, Harold, and his wife, Betty, who lived - with their lovely daughter, Lesley - in a large flat in St. John's Wood and spent several pleasant evenings with them. Harold had told me, when I met him by remarkable co-incidence in Calcutta, during the war, that he thought of opening a garage with another chap he'd met in the RAF. However, such ideas had vanished rapidly when he obtained a prestigious position in Great Universal Stores whose owner was, I believe, connected with his wife's family. And I gathered later that he was highly regarded there.

I saw very little of the Schmidts, our second cousins, with whom we had been in quite frequent contact before the war. The eldest, Ruby, had done brilliantly at maths, and eventually secured a top post in traffic control in the civil service. But I only met him once, after the war, at my sister's house and the only item of conversation I can remember was his saying, when he discovered that I was a teacher: "Of course, you're a member of the National Association Of Schoolmasters." I was "of course" a member of the NUT and the NAS were, at that time, our deadly rivals!

There is no space here to give details of my re-association with my other relatives and pre-war acquaintances and so I come to the correspondence and eventual personal meeting with my old American friend and comrade, Harold Leventhal. I had met him in Calcutta and we were both frequent visitors to the Sircars, the wonderful Bengali family I have already mentioned,. Harold wrote to say that he was visiting Britain and would call on me. After the war he had set up as an impresario for folk singers and, having "discovered" Pete Seeger, went on from strength to strength. In short he'd become a successful businessman but promoting progressive artistes. He arrived in London, as promised, and it was a great joy to introduce him to my parents, whose background was very similar to that of his parents. He had married and already had two little daughters. We talked far into the night and I discovered that he had become somewhat disillusioned with left politics, though he still stoutly maintained his "progressive" credentials, and I detected a distinct leaning towards Zionism which, incidentally, I have noticed often happens to Jewish comrades who left the Party for a variety of reasons, some of which I *now* realise were perfectly valid.

I also discovered that he regularly went back to India, on business, and so met Suman Sircar and his family again. He told Suman about his correspondence, meeting and exchange of views with me. This encouraged Suman to write to me and thus began an exchange of letters between us that only ended with his untimely death many years later. Sadly, I was never able to visit India, myself, which I would dearly loved to have done, to meet Suman again and all his relatives with whom I had such a close and friendly relationship whilst I was there.

As my interest in the theatre was as strong as ever, my friends and I were frequent visitors to West End shows. One play I remember very vividly, because I got to know an actor in it, was *Anna Lucasta*, an American drama about a Black family in New York and the emotional trauma between the generations. The play was originally written about a Polish family but altered to accommodate the totally Black group who produced it. I went with my old friend, Mick Naughton, who knew the actor playing the father who was meant to be about fifty in the play but who turned out to be a handsome young man of thirty-five. His name was Frank Silvera and we were soon good friends.

I learnt a lot about race relations in the USA from him. He told me he was looked on as a "yellow" Negro (incidentally, Negro was an acceptable term at the time, though it has lately fallen into disrepute). His skin was the colour of parchment, hence the expression. Of course, his paleness was no protection against racism. He was an actor of a very high calibre and I later saw him in a Hollywood film, *Viva Zapata!* I think it was. He was also a wonderful reciter of verse. Mick and I attended charity performances he gave and this was where I first heard a wonderful poem called *Strong Men*. We were privileged to stand in the wings and watch from behind the scenes. As Sybil Thorndyke was also in the show and recited a delightful children's poem, I was doubly thrilled.

Two other events that touched my life at the time should, perhaps, also be mentioned. The first was connected with Skiffle. This was a typical craze that "came up from the streets". It was discovered that an old-fashioned washboard (sometimes referred to as a skiffle) could be used as a musical instrument. It was a craze that spread from America and became immensely popular over here. Groups sprang up all over the place and a few of them hit the bright lights. But most were content to perform at small, intimate gigs. It was at one of these that I officiated and I enjoyed it tremendously, especially the rapport that developed between the youngsters performing and me. I believe it was a kind of competition but, fortunately, I wasn't called upon to judge.

The other significant event in my life, which occurred when I was teaching at Holloway, was the purchase of my first post-war car. It was a Morris 12, more or less streamlined and it added greatly to my quality of life. Prior to this, I had sometimes gone down to Peter Borin to see if I could cadge a lift to school when I was late, as he passed near the school on his way to work. Now I was booted and spurred, myself. It was also very convenient for taking my parents around. All in all, it gave me a degree of independence and really propelled me into the post-war era.

It was about this time that I was informed that my divorce proceedings were to come to court so I travelled to Birmingham and went through a somewhat farcical hearing during which a few facts were "stretched" a little and I was granted a divorce, to take effect a year from that date. And that was that. One positive result was that I stayed with the hospitable Greens, Larry and Len, and Larry and I chewed over our college days together.

POLITICS

Now that I was back in London I took up my political activity where I had left off some nine years ago, in those memorable days before the war. Now that the Nazis had been defeated was certainly not the time to abandon the struggle for a lasting peace and social justice. In the Temple Fortune branch of the Party I was working alongside a whole new group of comrades. Max Egelnik, whom I'd known before the war as a "sympathiser" was now an activist, a full-time Party worker and secretary of the Hendon Borough. He lived at the top end of our street and so I saw a lot of him and his wife, Sadie as they organised not only meetings but also quite frequent socials at their house.

Soon after I arrived, a young ex-serviceman came to live in the area called Wolf Wayne. Wolf had been through a number of adventures in the army and was already a seasoned campaigner, especially in the anti-fascist movement. I should say here that, despite all that had been revealed about Nazi beastliness, the fascist movement sprang up again in Britain and elsewhere with all the brazen impudence of the blind bigot. Wolf was a member of the "43 Group", made up of ex-servicemen determined to stamp out any resurgence of fascism, which they had risked their lives to defeat during the war. The group was formed as a result of dissatisfaction within the ranks of the official Association of Jewish Ex-servicemen whose attitude to this resurgence in Britain was: "Leave them alone, give them no publicity and they'll fade away!" Forty-three members resigned and formed their own group, hence the name.

Another local comrade was Joan Thompson, widow of a lawyer who had been well known in defending progressives who had come into conflict with the law. Which reminds me that there was a whole number of lawyers in our movement, indeed, our branch boasted three, two lawyers and even one barrister, Dick Freeman. This latter was a very interesting case. He stemmed from the upper middle class (his father was a consultant) had been to Public School but was fired with revolutionary zeal at Oxford, where, as chairman of the Union, he had presided over the meeting that had passed the famous anti-war resolution.

Perhaps the most interesting family that moved into the area a few years later were the Amiels, Barry, his wife, Nicky, their two sons, Steve and Jonathan and a gorgeous little cherub of a daughter, Rebecca. These were later to be joined by another girl, Elizabeth. Barry's family were well known for their good works, especially during the war. Barry was one of the lawmen, referred to above. He was also highly talented in other directions. Nicky was not only a remarkable mother, she was also well organised, knew what she wanted and where she was going and had tremendous empathy with others. Their house became a centre for meetings, socials and parties and we became close friends.

The Amiels circa 1960

The most important campaign undertaken by the progressive movement in general and the Party in particular was for world peace. It may seem strange, looking back, that so soon after the triumphant conclusion of the most destructive war in history, peace was again in danger. But the Cold War had begun when we were still surrounded by the painful results of the hot war. Many of us feel that its origins are to be seen in Churchill's speech at Fulton in the USA, when he repeated the Goebbels phrase: "an iron curtain is stretching across Europe" but it really began in 1917, when the Russian Revolution swept away the rotting Czarist system and seemed to threaten world capitalism with the promise of "rule by the workers".

There are, of course, many conflicting views on that subject but one thing is clear; almost immediately after the war against fascism, the world stood before the awful possibility of another, even more devastating conflagration and this time with weapons on both sides that could - and almost certainly would - destroy our civilisation. Thus a considerable section of public opinion saw it as the most urgent task to rid the world of these awesome weapons, so that the belligerence born of their possession and the horrifying dangers of their use would, at least, be removed.

In 1950, the World Peace Conference organised the Stockholm Peace appeal. This was a petition, to be presented to the governments of the five major powers (UK, USA, France, China, USSR) demanding, I quote: "unconditional prohibition of atomic weapons." That the Appeal was organised in Britain by the British Peace Committee that, according to the media, was under Communist influence if it was not, indeed, a "Communist front" organisation, certainly prejudiced many sincere anti-bomb people against it. Nonetheless, we gathered over a million signatures, by door-to-door canvassing, street collections and promotion at meetings. Worldwide, tens of millions signed up.

The Soviet Union declared itself willing to abandon its nuclear arsenal totally, if the other nuclear powers would do the same. Churchill's response was: "You can do what you like. We're holding on to ours!" And then came the H-bomb, with a destructive force that made the Hiroshima bomb seem like a toy. Our argument was that these weapons know no national boundaries and the explosion of just one of them (and a much greater proliferation was likely) would poison the atmosphere for generations to come - and not only in the "enemy" country, but throughout the world. What sort of "defence" was that?

The arguments and the campaigning continued, with anti-bomb sentiment garnering very considerable support until, in 1958, the Campaign for Nuclear Disarmament (CND) was set up by, among others, several prestigious personalities: Bertrand Russell (the philosopher), J. B. Priestley (the novelist), Canon Collins, Julian Huxley (the scientist), Michael Foot(!) and a number of others. My own part in all these activities was to support marches and the earlier petition. I went round knocking on doors in the Temple Fortune, Hampstead Garden Suburb area and generally did the footwork as well as the arguing.

Another campaign we ran was against German re-armament. Within a few years of the successful collaboration between the West and the Soviet Union to destroy German imperial ambitions and their mastery of most of Europe, the West was contemplating arming this former enemy (now "democratic" of course) to defend us against the "danger" of a Soviet attack. What an irony! The SU had lost 30 million citizens, had its European territory devastated twice and was struggling to rebuild its infrastructure and produce enough consumer goods for its people, and yet - it was a "threat".

I can well remember heading a poster parade on the issue through Golders Green Rd. on a Saturday morning. But the Americans were implacable. West Germany (the Federal Republic) was re-armed and, shortly afterwards the German Democratic Republic responded, establishing what it called *Die Volksarmee* (the People's Army). Thus the Cold War was taken a step further and I am convinced that the enormous burden of military expenditure, both in the GDR and the SU, trying to match the USA's military might, was one of the factors that led to the downfall of the whole system. Maybe this was the intention in the first place? But then, I am incurably suspicious.

I also began to make other new acquaintances. Locally, I became very friendly with a comrade who lived round the corner, called Peter Borin. Peter (originally Percy Borinsky) was short, dark and Semitic in appearance. He also displayed many of the characteristics often associated with our people. He was intensely musical and had trained as a singer with a well-known musician. This was a leisure pursuit, however; he made his living as a cutter of ladies' coats, in his own workshop near Liverpool St., where he employed some twenty skilled tailoring workers to do the sewing, pressing etc.

He had considerable practical ability, understood and was able to do elementary repairs to all the complicated machines in his workshop. Added to this, his medical knowledge was quite considerable for a layman, although this was accompanied by certain hypochondriac tendencies. We went around a great deal together: two fancy-free bachelors. He had an old car with very tricky gears but it served us well. We must have seemed a very odd couple, considering our contrasting build but we actually had much in common, apart from our single state. Although not musical, like him, I enjoyed good music as well as good food and good company. And then there was our political affinity, which had brought us together in the first place. Eventually, however, Cold War propaganda began to get to him and, over the years, his left-wing ardour cooled considerably.

Best man at Pete Borin's wedding

Whilst I was still in my anti-marriage mode, Peter was pining for a mate, so when he was introduced to Bonnie, dining in a restaurant with an old friend of his, they started a relationship which eventually led to marriage. I acted as best man. Peter and I looked somewhat sheepish in morning dress as you can see in the photograph of the wedding group above. Far from showing me the door - often the fate of "best friends" when one of them gets married - Bonnie was hospitality itself and I became a frequent visitor to their house and beneficiary of Bonnie's superb cooking.

One development in which I was personally involved that arose from the establishment of People's Democracies, later socialist or "Iron Curtain" countries, was the setting up of Friendship Societies by their sympathisers in Britain. I joined the British-Czech Friendship Society in 1948 and went on a visit they organised to Czechoslovakia. The main purpose of the trip was to do some logging in the *Riesengebirge* (Giant Mountains) but also to get to know the natives and generally to enjoy ourselves. We were to be provided with food and lodgings and, after the task was completed, with sufficient cash to go and have a rare old time in Prague.

One of those who apprised me of this trip was my old friend and comrade, Mick Naughton, of Unity Theatre, as he was going, too. We were a very friendly crowd of young men and women and we developed a wonderful camaraderie and the sort of high spirits that joint work on a project of that type always engenders. There were cultural events every evening, with the Czechs putting on performances of their fascinating folk dancing and singing. I'm afraid all we could respond with was "There is a Tavern" and "She'll be coming down the Mountain..."

Other events connected with the socialist countries were the biennial World Youth Festivals. The first one, held (I think) in Prague was in 1947. The second one, in which I participated, took place in Budapest, in 1949. True, I was already 33 and no longer in the first flush of youth but that didn't seem to matter. We were housed in a school and extremely well fed. The festival consisted of a grand opening ceremony, in which the "delegations" from each country paraded round a stadium, carrying their country's flag. This was followed by a welcoming speech by their prime minister and several other speeches. One lasting memory is of the Americans in the parade, led by a black female and a white male delegate carrying their flag together. This aroused an enormous cheer.

The next festival, in 1951, was held in East Berlin, capital of the German Democratic Republic. This occasion has a special place in my memory and no doubt of all the other Britons travelling there, because of the special circumstances associated with the journey. The train took us through Innsbruck, at that time in the American zone of Austria - and that was where the trouble started.

We had been travelling for about half an hour when the train was boarded by American soldiers who proceeded to order all festival participants off the train on the flimsy excuse that we didn't have a green card which, it was maintained, the Russians were demanding for all those entering *their* zone. We were compelled to remain on the lines all night, constantly menaced by shunting trains and without food or water. Next morning the American soldiers ordered us to get on a train to take us back. Some complied but most of us refused, demanding to be allowed to proceed to Berlin.

During the hiatus which followed, an interesting debate took place between Alan Bush, who had boarded the train with his young daughter, and

Wolf Wayne, already mentioned as a local comrade and friend, who was still standing on the railway lines, as to the wisdom or otherwise of complying with the American command. It should be noted that Wolf had naturally fallen into a leadership role and had even negotiated, unsuccessfully, with the American commander. His discussion with Alan became quite theoretical and must have been incomprehensible to the soldiers standing around.

Soon after, however, those of us still on the lines were herded back onto the train at bayonet point and returned to Innsbruck. The leaders of the delegation were no greenhorns when it came to political action and a great demonstration was organised through the town to the British consulate. We were accompanied by the French delegates, who had apparently been treated in the same way, and a colourful event it turned out to be. Holding hands, they made a huge ring around us, moving forwards at the same time (quite a skilful manoeuvre) and chanting "Pour la paix, à Berlin! ". The spirit of comradeship sent a warm glow through all of us.

The public interest all this aroused apparently reached England and, so I'm told, several papers carried reports of the incident. Our problem was eventually solved when the local comrades organised coaches to take us, by devious routes, to the border of the Soviet Zone, where we were ushered through with little ceremony and were, at last, on our way to Berlin.

This festival was also a great success. One of the high points was when we were all mustered in a large square in the middle of East Berlin, to listen to speeches, first by Walter Ulbricht and then by leaders of the various delegations. Our own Bert Pockney, tall and ginger-haired, made quite an impression. This experience was important in one other very significant respect: it aroused my interest in the GDR and this played a crucial role in my life, which will be explained in considerable detail in a later chapter.

The last festival that I attended, in Bucharest in 1953, was associated with Unity Theatre, with which I got into contact soon after I returned to London. They were sending a group to the festival to perform a kind of mime to music. It was particularly memorable for me because one of the members who came was Lionel Bart, later to become quite a celebrity as composer and scriptwriter of *Fings ain't wot they used to be* and *Oliver,* both of which had such a great success in the West End and elsewhere. Lionel, an East End cockney with a huge beak of a nose, which he later had "adjusted", had also written lyrics for Unity musicals. After the war, many Unity players had turned professional and some of them became household names, two in particular. One was Alfie Bass, an outstanding Tevye in *Fiddler on the Roof* , and Bill Owen, of *Last of the Summer Wine*.

Talking of theatrical events, in 1956, Nikita Khruschev, who had become leader of the Soviet Union after Stalin's death, made a speech to the 20th Congress of the Soviet Communist Party which changed the whole political landscape and precipitated events whose long-term results we have only witnessed in the last ten years. Put briefly, he made most serious accusations against Stalin, giving details of the latter's megalomaniac activities resulting in gross and criminal breaches of the very constitution that bore his name! The stories of good, loyal comrades being sent to prison camps, the notorious gulags, which we had always denied and condemned as "enemy propaganda", turned out to be true. The rumours were, no doubt, exaggerated by the hostile media, but the substance was there. The Observer printed a version of the speech that the Party accepted as accurate and this opened up wounds that had been festering in the Party for some time.

The divisions were between those who, on the one hand, felt that our criticism of the SU did not go far enough and that the EC's reaction was inadequate and those, on the other hand, for whom the Soviet Union, the world bastion of socialism, was sacrosanct and who felt that, even where we disagreed, this should not be in public, that we should constitute ourselves as a defensive wall, "in the face of the enemy". Some left the Party in disgust and many ex-comrades became the bitterest critics both of the SU and of the Party.

Others remained in the Party only to fight for it to cut itself adrift from the Soviet Union and, incidentally, change a whole lot of its policies and, for some, its whole constitution. One big problem centred on the question of information. Khrushchev's revelations could hardly be questioned, considering his position. But what of the "revelations" in the British media, known to be implacably hostile to the SU? It was because of this hostility of "the class enemy" that I, along with many others, had been reluctant to believe their stories of persecution and imprisonment, but also of poor living standards, with which the newspapers were peppered.

Another bone of contention related to the question of class. Marx, we held, had "laid bare" the inescapable struggle between the ruling class - the capitalists - and the working class, whom they exploited, robbed of the "values" which they had produced. In the post-war period, however, many workers, even unskilled ones, had an income enabling them not only to acquire a high level of consumer and other goods, especially cars (and, indeed, their own homes) but also to take holidays abroad and even, in some cases, own property abroad.

In this new situation, it was held by some, how could you talk of "downtrodden" workers struggling against exploitation? These comrades were not, at that point, openly coming out with the suggestion that we abandon socialism as an aim but they were, at least, suggesting that it was not currently "on the agenda". This was the situation within and around the Party when a series of events occurred which turned out to be another watershed in my life.

ACADEMIA IN THE GDR - A DECISIVE STEP

In the summer of 1957, I heard of a group of teachers who were going to the German Democratic Republic. This was a fortnight's trip, organised by Dorothy Diamond, a very experienced Grammar School teacher of science, for the purpose of setting up a summer school for teachers of English. It was to be held in Weimar, a beautiful old town, associated with the name of Goethe, in the same way that Stratford is associated with Shakespeare. It also had a place in history, giving its name to the republic that was set up after the overthrow of the Kaiser at the end of the First World War.

My fellow participants were an interesting lot. Apart from Dorothy, a live spark if ever there was one, there was Harold Rosen, a lecturer in English at a teachers' Training College and his wife, Connie, also a teacher and their two sons, one of whom, Michael, is now a well known broadcaster and writer of children's fiction. There were many other congenial colleagues on the trip and we formed a very sociable group, especially when we all went, with our students, to the local hostelry. I think we disabused any Germans who might have laboured under the impression that the English were stiff and staid, of any such idea. In fact, we probably made a noisy nuisance of ourselves on many occasions.

All in all, the summer school was voted a roaring success and I'm sure we helped to "anglicise" the English of those GDR teachers, to the great benefit of their pupils. Whilst we were there, we were visited by a representative of Leipzig University - Karl Marx University, to give it its official name. He made a brief statement to the effect that the university was seeking a *Lektor* (assistant) for English, to work alongside their German colleagues in the English and Interpreters' Institutes. Were any of those present interested? There were no immediate takers but I'm certain that we were all doing some furious thinking. On my return home, my furious thinking turned to action. I had been feeling stale and somewhat frustrated for some time before the GDR trip and now there seemed a chance to try something different.

By working in Leipzig I would, firstly, be doing what I enjoy above all else, practising my skills in the language and passing them on to eager students; secondly, I would be helping a socialist country; thirdly, I would get out of the rut I felt myself in, absorb the culture of another country about which I only previously knew from books and make new friends and, fourthly, I'd have a chance to teach at university level - an opportunity I was unlikely to have in Britain. To be brief: I applied. In the event, a number of other advantages accrued, as will be seen, which I had only vaguely considered, if at all. I received a very welcoming letter, translated for me by Dorothy, in reply to my application, in which they gave me a general idea about my duties and the salary I would receive but added that they could give me *nähere Einzelheiten* (a more detailed explanation) on the spot, when I arrived. The appointment was to be for one year.

Monument to the Battle of the Nations: "A hideous Teutonic pile."

I had a number of matters to settle before I could take up the post in Leipzig. Firstly, of course, I had to make an arrangement with the LCC, my employers, to hold my post open for a year. They were prepared to do this and my Headmaster was kind enough to say that, even if I stayed longer, he would see to it that I could come back to the school. Next, I had to sell my car. As I was not selling it in part exchange for another one, I got a very poor deal. Finally, I had to pack. This was not as easy as it sounds. I wasn't going for a fortnight's holiday but for a whole year. Packing my immediate needs was simple enough. All the other articles I wanted to have with me over there were crated by a shipping company and despatched separately. Considerable quantities of Nescafé and tea were included!

By great good fortune, a couple of friends were driving to Czechoslovakia on holiday that summer and invited me to share the driving and join their trip. From there we could cross over into the GDR and they could drive me to Leipzig. I shall not dwell on the Czech holiday, at Marianske Lazhne (Marienbad to the Germans) except to say that we enjoyed it immensely, especially our visit to a collective farm where we were wined and dined in the local inn and I had to drive the car back to our hotel because my companion was overcome by an excess of celebrating.

Our first target was not Leipzig but Karl-Marx Stadt, and on to Weissenfels, where I was to meet a Herr Hückel, the very same man who had spoken to us in Weimar. As K-M Stadt did not seem to be marked on the otherwise excellent AA map, we had some difficulty until it dawned on us that the AA, with a sturdy

Cold War attitude, had omitted to re-name it and insisted on calling it by its pre-war name, Chemnitz. Having overcome that little difficulty we passed through the city and made our way to Herr Hückel's house where I put up for the night, after having deposited the other two in a small local hotel.

The next day we all travelled to Leipzig, where my new colleague showed us the sights. The main one was the *Völkerschlachtdenkmal* (monument to the Battle of the Nations ie the defeat of Napoleon). This is a massive, hideous, Teutonic pile but, like Nelson's Column, it simply has to be seen by all visitors. My friends departed at this stage and I was taken to my lodgings, which were to be my home for most of my stay in the GDR. Of course, I didn't know this at the time. The appearance of the building was impressive. It looked like a Spanish riding school and had been built by wealthy furriers, Leipzig having been the main centre for the fur trade.

It housed visiting academics, mainly professors, and was called *Haus der Wissenschaftler* (freely translated: University House) and popularly known as HdW. Right opposite was the Dimitrov Museum, where the trial of the famous Bulgarian Communist was held in the early Nazi period. He and others were accused of setting fire to the Reichstag but he defied Goering in open court and was eventually acquitted as a result of his own stand and a worldwide campaign in his defence. The museum contains a tape of his angry exchanges with Goering.

Soon after my arrival in the GDR.

Shortly after I had settled in, a note arrived from a Dr. Brüning, welcoming me to Leipzig and to the university and indicating that he was looking forward to fruitful co-operation with me, unless I changed my mind, which he sincerely hoped I would not. He asked me to meet him at the English Institute the next day, in his office. When I arrived he was sitting behind his desk and he rose to meet me. I was confronted by a tall, bespectacled, rather beefy figure who greeted me warmly. After a few preliminary remarks on both sides, it very quickly became clear that he wanted to establish a friendly relationship right from the start. His name was Eberhardt but, he told me, his friends called him Ebs and he'd like it if I did the same. I told him to call me Len, so that informal mode of address was settled and we got down to business.

He outlined my duties in some detail. I was to work in the Interpreters' Institute, training interpreters and translators, and in the English Institute whose students were set to become either teachers or academics or to work in publishing and similar enterprises. My main value to the university and thus to the GDR was in turning the students' passive knowledge of the language (often very good indeed) into idiomatic, colloquial English. But perhaps my most important task of all was to attend to their pronunciation and intonation, to familiarise them with the *sound* of English, as spoken by the native. The tradition in most foreign countries is to teach English in what used to be called "received" pronunciation, which means an educated, southern one, though this is being more and more challenged, for obvious reasons.

My first day and my first group of students were quite an experience. I was given the more advanced students, Years Four and Five, whose grasp of the essentials of *passive* English was held to be sufficiently secure to benefit from my attempts to *activise* their speech. I had no idea what their standard of English was and so I had prepared a text, simply to hear their pronunciation that, to me, is all-important. I wanted to get them *into* the language, to get the *feel* of it. It must be remembered that, unlike students in West Germany, they had no opportunity to travel to countries where English was spoken as the native language. I was some sort of living resource for them and, I learned later, they were very grateful. As I listened, a certain pattern emerged. Some sounds were particularly difficult for them and sounded more like German than English and their accentuation tended to follow the German, too.

I realised that my task was to break their speech habits of a lifetime and that this would not be easy. When speaking, I always slightly exaggerated especially the vowel sounds and the intonation. I reckoned I could easily tone this down and make it more natural, once they had mastered the differences and it was these I insisted on, even going so far as to mimic their speech and follow it immediately with my own. I noticed with satisfaction that they were all busily taking down notes.

My next meeting was with Prof. Martin, Head of the institute and referred to by the lecturers as "the Old Man". He was large and rotund, with big cheeks in a round face. He had a jovial manner and some acquaintanceship with England and his big pale blue eyes looked me over with a friendly gaze. Like Ebs, he told me how glad he was that I had come and said he was sure I would be successful with the students. He said he would like to see me once a week to discuss progress and any problems that might arise. It seemed he was also planning to entertain me at his home from time to time.

The Interpreters' Institute was my next port of call and I noticed immediately a certain indefinable difference in the students, especially the girls. An interpreter's personality has to be somewhat different from that of a teacher or an academic and it was clear that they saw themselves, and were seen, as potential representatives of their country at international events, both political and commercial so, not to put a fine point on it, appearance was important. Whether or not this had been taken into account when they were accepted into the institute, I do not know, but the atmosphere was altogether racier and more electric than in the English Institute and, for some inexplicable reason, I seemed to notice all the pretty girls.

Also, there were several languages taught there in addition to English: Russian, French and Spanish and there were Russian students there, as well. Indeed, I had one class of them. I noted that their difficulties were different from those of the German students and I altered my techniques accordingly. Another class was composed entirely of army officers in training, a very pleasant lot indeed, charming, unassuming and very hardworking.

Apart from the lectures to individual classes, I was also asked to give a regular lecture to the whole institute, on: Life in England. I gave twelve of these, all in all, and I still have the taped recordings of them. I sometimes amuse myself by playing them back and notice how slowly I spoke and how I emphasised certain points, sometimes repeating a word or a phrase. I have first-hand evidence that these talks were appreciated by the students and staff.

Although surrounded by Germans it was not easy to learn the language. Most of my contacts wanted to use me as a living resource for their studies, most of which were in English. I was there to help them practise their English, not for me to practise German. So my acquisition of German was slow and tortuous, though I did have a small smattering of it before I went. I was, however, extensively used for editing translations done by my colleagues. I became a kind of guru to whom all English linguistic problems were referred. Quite an exalted position really but I thoroughly enjoyed the work of correcting or, in most cases, improving their translations and, indeed, their speech.

I suppose the most prestigious work I edited was a colleague's translation of: "An Illustrated History of Education". I was, after all, an educationist of sorts and it gave me great pleasure to anglicise his draft and, moreover, as I had the original German text in front of me, it also helped to improve my mastery of the language. The pictures were there to guide me, too, and I think I made a passable job of it. There was another English chap in Leipzig but he was rather reclusive. His name was George Baurley, a Yorkshireman, small and rather thin, with glasses and somewhat on the intellectual side. He and I met from time to time and rubbed our ideas together. Although I greatly valued my German contacts, I found it refreshing to talk to a fellow Englishman now and again.

I did gradually improve my German in a number of different ways and became quite fluent in the end, though I still made - and make - many grammatical mistakes. However, my greater grasp of the language meant that I could do translating, myself, and as this became more and more apparent, translating commissions began to come in. I did a number of translations for the English edition of their export magazine, work that I continued by mail after I returned to England. I translated advertisements as well for use during the Leipzig Fair.

I was particularly proud of a solution I found for a description of a piece of furniture that, though it could be folded away, was nonetheless comfortable (or so they claimed!). It was the simple slogan: Rest Assured! The original German for this was a stodgy attempt to laud their product which, if translated literally, would have sunk like a lead balloon. Imagine my surprise to see that same slogan used in an advert in England, many years later. Of course, it was just a co-incidence. My major work, however, was a translation of the book they published to celebrate 800 years of the Leipzig Fair.

A colleague from the Foreign Languages Department, mentioned above, suggested to me that we should jointly produce a picture book in the series on foreign lands which were being published at the time. He was Ernst Bartsch, a very enterprising young man. The book was to be called: *Grossbritannien* i.e. Great Britain (what else?). I set about collecting photographs from a wide variety of sources in England and I must say I received friendly collaboration wherever I went. The book lies in front of me now, in the German translation, of course. They had no intention of selling it in the UK.

There is a superb coloured picture of the Houses of Parliament and Westminster Bridge on the front cover and, inside, a preface by the Dean of Canterbury to whom I had sent both the text of the introduction and the captions of all the pictures. From these he'd got a good idea of the book's contents. He called the book "excellent" and praised the breadth of vision in the pictures I had chosen. He said it was not only a fascinating book, but also an honest book, showing all sides of life in Britain. He also said that he wished he were a good photographer or artist, so that he could have given the British people a similar picture of Russia or China. The book sold well but shortage of materials precluded a second edition.

Another publisher approached me to do a couple of textbooks for learners, which could also be used as "Teach Yourself" books. I was paired with a German colleague and my main role was to supply the texts, in English, which he would then render into German. I also had to supervise his grammatical and linguistic explanations. He was a Dr. Bernhard Schindler, who had profited from his years as a prisoner-of-war, to perfect and develop his school-English. He was thin and wiry, had penetrating grey-blue eyes and a certain nervousness that I noticed characterised many Germans who had been through the traumatic experience of Nazism, war and post-war chaos.

Although we produced a first edition which sold out quite quickly, he proved a most unreliable partner, never delivering his part of the work on time and quarrelling and prevaricating with the publishers when they complained, so that, eventually, he was "sacked" and another more reliable co-author was found, namely, Hans Löffler. Hans and I developed a close personal and professional friendship. Although he was somewhat slower than the volatile Bernhard, he worked very hard, always delivered on time and was full of ideas on how to improve on the original work.

The two-volume work was called *Taschenlehrbuch Englisch - Teil I und II* (Pocket Textbook - English - Part I and II). During its composition, Hans had used many of the texts with his First Year groups and we had modified and changed some of the material as a result of his experiences of actually using it. Partly, no doubt, as a result of this very practical method of constructing a textbook, the work was highly successful. And it became routine to publish reprints, and sometimes revised versions, on an almost annual basis.

After this, Hans suggested that we should do a book on synonyms. I readily agreed and we set to work on what was to be a difficult but fascinating investigation into words of similar meanings and, even more difficult, explaining the exact nuances of difference in each case. Try, for example, explaining the difference between big and large, and you'll see what I mean. We first called the book: *English synonyms and how to use them,* which we later changed to *English synonyms at work.* When I returned to England we continued to work on the book and published the first edition. Later, we produced revised versions and I still have the extensive exchange of letters and documents in which Hans and I hammered the whole thing out..

The book was an instant success, receiving laudatory reviews, even in West Germany. Strangely enough, its best review appeared in the book review section of the West German army publication, which finished with the comment::*..eine feine abgerundete Sache* (..a fine, well-crafted work). It is still being marketed by Langenscheidt, in the now united Germany, under the new title of *Find the right word.* Another book I produced, this time in collaboration with George Baurley, was a German/English/German picture dictionary. It was a very modest attempt to match the West German Duden. The dictionary, I have it before me, is divided into subjects, Plants, Animals, Human Body etc. Of course, no-one can specialise in all these fields, so I used my many contacts in England to help me. I even contacted the German teacher in my old Comprehensive School, who just happened to be an expert on mushrooms!

One of my monitoring duties at the English Institute was to observe the lessons of my teacher students when they were on school practice. One such visit resulted in a friendship that has lasted to this day. It so happened that this class (equivalent to our Year Twelve) were to have their "Day in Production" the following week. I should explain that one excellent practice laid down in the

GDR's educational plans, was to visit a local firm (or farm, in the case of country schools), such as a factory or store or workshop, and take part in the work, much like our work-experience scheme but for all pupils, once a week, in their last four years at school.

The purpose was not necessarily to recruit them for that firm but to give them direct experience of the world of work, let them know from their own experience just who was creating the wealth that paid for their schooling and, even more important, just what effort was required for this. This was especially important precisely for those who might go on to higher education and never see the inside of a factory again in their lives.

Each of these specially chosen firms had to have a mentor, a skilled worker responsible for the youngsters whilst they were on the premises. This was a job requiring the utmost sensitivity towards and rapport with young people. They had to show them what discipline was involved in everyday work but, on the other hand, not put them off or be patronising. I can only say, from my own experience, that it seemed to work. I asked the pupils about it and their response was educative. Some, especially from a "middle-class" i.e. professional or managerial background, admitted to misgivings before they started, although some were glad at this relief from school formalities, right from the start. After three years experience of the scheme, almost all welcomed it and felt that they derived some benefit from it.

The class in question were assigned to the *Dimitroffkraftwerk* (Dimitrov power station) and the chap in charge of them was a certain Martin Richter. It so happened that his son, Roland, was actually in the class. I had a long chat with Herr Richter, my German was passable by this time. We hit it off rather well and were soon on first-name terms. Although, naturally, our lives had been very different in most respects, we had both come to a similar outlook on life and our exchange of personal information was enlivened by banter and bonhomie.

Back at school it was always my habit - apparently greatly appreciated by staff and pupils - to say a few words to the class after the lesson was over. I brought into the classroom a whiff of the West, about which the pupils were always intrigued. They were all around eighteen years of age and, on one occasion, when I had said my piece, one of the pupils stood up and thanked me and, at the same time, invited me to join them in a camping expedition they were having that weekend. I readily agreed and found, to my delight, that Martin was coming, too. Despite the discomforts - there was a plague of horseflies in the area! - I thoroughly enjoyed the company of the young people. They confided their ambitions and plans, as well as their anxieties, in this relaxed, informal atmosphere.

At one point, I went off with Martin and our extensive conversation led to a friendship which has lasted to the present day. I was invited to his home, met his hospitable wife, Elfriede, and Roland and his sister, Dagmar, and have enjoyed their kind hospitality ever since.

The Richter family when I first knew them.

There is no doubt that this professional experience of Higher Education gave me insights into academic life and the problems associated with teaching older adolescents and, indeed, adults that I should not otherwise have had and therefore added to my store of expertise. I am especially grateful for the opportunity to write textbooks and, of course, to learn a foreign language in the country in which it is spoken. The other benefits of my GDR activities will appear as the story unfolds.

SOCIAL AND PROFESSIONAL LIFE IN THE GDR

Even for teachers and lecturers, life is not all work. There is always room for entertainment and relaxation. Indeed, even work can sometimes be entertaining, if not necessarily relaxing. In the GDR I had plenty of time to enjoy myself and also to entertain others. Most of the colleagues were congenial and ready for fun and I never felt restrained in their presence.

The university had a *Fremdsprachenabteilung* (Foreign Languages Department) whose task it was to teach foreign languages to students specialising in other disciplines. I had the very pleasant job of holding seminars with the staff of this department and thereby met some very interesting colleagues. We took it quite light-heartedly and I mainly dealt with their queries, which ranged over a very wide area, way beyond mere language. We usually met either in my room or a room in the university but occasionally held the seminar in some hostelry or restaurant, where coffee and cakes "made the medicine go down in a most delightful way"!

One of these lecturers, a Herr Lee, collected songs current in the movement, like *Old Man Atom* and I helped him to transcribe them on the typewriter. Another elderly colleague, Dr. Beyer, was a great joker and we got on famously, sometimes holding individual "seminars" in the coffee shop (I do love those German pastries!). But the most interesting of these colleagues was a Hans-Gert Kupferschmidt, whose English was very advanced indeed and who gave English lessons to the medical students. Later, he studied medicine, himself, and is now an experienced practitioner. We remained on friendly terms

Ebs soon introduced me to his wife, Usch, and his two small children and I became a regular visitor to their home where I was fed and made very welcome, and I soon became almost a part of the family. I sometimes invited them to my room in Haus der Wissenschaftler. Entertaining of the kind I did was comparatively easy. I just bought sliced cheese and *Wurst* (sausage) of various kinds, also sliced, from the local *Lebensmittel* (grocery) shop. There was a bread-slicing machine in the kitchen and *voilà,* there was the basis for an excellent supper. I also succeeded in corrupting them into drinking tea with milk(!) instead of their interminable coffee.

Later on, Ebs introduced me to his two closest colleagues: Albrecht Neubert who, like Ebs, was on his first doctorate, and Karl-Heinz Schönfelder, nicknamed Belly, who was already a professor at Halle University. He seemed very spruce and fit to me, so I don't know the origin of his nickname. Ebs was an Americanist, delving into the protest and progressive literature of the Thirties. Belly was working on similar lines and his specialism was Jack London. Albrecht had opted for linguistics, of which he later became an internationally known expert, invited to seminars and lectures all over the world, including the USA. He also took me home to meet his wife. Doris, and their flat, too, became a home from home for me. I was and am deeply impressed by the friendship and hospitality shown to me by these two colleagues and their wives which has continued to the present day.

Werner Hückel, the man who'd introduced me to the university in the first place, was a strange and somewhat nerve-wracked individual. His movements were jerky and his speech was explosive. This meant that, despite his quite good command of English (he was head of the department) when he spoke it, as he did all the time to me, of course, it sounded harsh and foreign. He didn't feel up to showing me Leipzig's night life, which he assumed I would want to experience, but told me that another colleague, Lothar Römer, who was away at the time, would be just the person to show me around.

I met Lothar shortly after he arrived back from a visit to India. He was short of stature, quite thickset and bubbling over with energy. His English was very fluent, if a bit over-colloquial and he was studying for his doctorate. The subject: *Use of the hyphen in English.* True to my informant's expectation, he became a frequent companion on evening jaunts to local nightspots where we partook of tasty snacks, both on the table and on the dance floor. I also visited him in his flat and had many a good meal, listening to the radio, or one of his records or watching television. I soon realised that he was many-talented linguistically. His grasp of the fundamentals of what was being said and his ability to render it rapidly in the other language, whether English or German, was phenomenal He also turned out to be a very effective and popular teacher.

From left to right: Myself, Lothar, Prof. Mayer, rector of the University. Between them, in the second row is Bernhard Schindler. c. 1960

I discovered this when he invited me to take part in some of his lectures. The format was a conversation between the two of us for which selected students had to act as interpreters. He knew how to provoke debate and kept the class in a constant state of amusement but forcing them to concentrate on the language used. I enjoyed these forays immensely and so did the students.

He was keen to keep fit and we often played tennis, early in the morning, before lectures. I was younger then! His contacts were extensive and he introduced me to the tennis coach at the GDR's prestigious *Deutsche Hochschule für Körperkultur* (German College of Physical Culture) who improved my game immensely. Incidentally, some of my students became lecturers in English at this college later on and enabled me to use the college's Olympic standard swimming pool, where they occasionally embroiled me in water polo, a game of whose practice and purpose I had only a rudimentary idea. Nonetheless, it was great fun, if somewhat tiring.

Ebs and Albrecht, my two closest friends in the GDR, frequently came to my room where, as I indicated above, I was able to entertain them with little or no trouble to myself. Making tea, the English way of course, has always been my delight: a pot with far more tea bags than any cafe will give you, a jug of milk and an extra pot of boiling water, plus a plateful of the delicious pastries only obtainable in Germany and particularly in Saxony. I still pine for them!

65

Every May Day, we university staff would get up early, swallow a hasty cup of coffee or tea and assemble for the march, which for us was always through the working-class area of Leipzig, apparently an old tradition that pre-dated the Hitler regime, when it was forbidden. After the march we three congregated in my room and I made, as far as possible, a good old English breakfast. This became a ceremony that was repeated for the whole seven years of my stay in the GDR. It was one of the many joint activities that cemented our friendship.

The German education system has two terms, known as semesters. Thus there are two major vacations, one at Christmas and the other in the summer. I always went back home to my parents at these times. On my first vacation, at the end of 1958, I had become so friendly with Ebs that I invited him to come home with me. My parents were delighted to see me and welcomed Ebs with open arms. It so happened that my friend and colleague, John Dixon, was having a New Years' Eve party that Ebs and I attended. It was a real baptism of fire for Ebs and he revelled in it, especially as everyone immediately called him by his nickname, something unheard of in Germany where the polite form of address is still used even among people who know each other quite well. Usually it is the older person who, at a suitable moment in their relationship, invites the other to use the familiar form of *Du*.

Ebs with my parents in our London garden. New Year 1960.

On our return to Leipzig, Ebs reported enthusiastically to his friends (and probably also to the authorities) about his experiences. On subsequent holidays Albrecht and Belly also came back with me. Once all three came together and Belly stayed with my friends, the Borins. It wasn't easy, even for academics, to get permission to travel to the West but each of these three were able to justify their visit, even after the building of The Wall, on the grounds that they were making contact with colleagues in British universities of benefit to the GDR . Ebs and Albrecht actually instigated an exchange scheme with Salford University that lasted throughout the life of the GDR.

Albrecht and Peter Weiss in Green Park, London.

Despite being domiciled "behind the Iron Curtain", I still maintained quite considerable connections with friends and acquaintances in England. Many people I knew came to the GDR for one reason or another. Alan Bush, the composer, was a fairly frequent visitor, as they produced his operas there. He always came to see me and we had many a pleasant chat over a cup of my famous tea. It was an opportunity to get to know him better than when I was in England and both of us were busy with other activities. On one occasion, Alan wrote to me and asked if I could arrange for a young friend of his, a mountaineer, to come to the GDR to do some climbing, as they have an area of sandstone mountains widely used by their own and foreign alpinists. Little did I realise at the time what an important part this area was to play in my life, a year or two later - and ever since - that it would indeed become my "second home"!

The young man was about seventeen and his name was Gavin Campbell (as an adult, he became well known as one of Esther Rantzen's researchers in "That's Life"). I managed to get his trip organised and got him lodgings, too. He turned out to be tall and powerfully built and eager for the fray. He thoroughly enjoyed his trip to *Die Sächsische Schweiz* (Saxon Switzerland) and went home full of enthusiasm for his experiences. On his arrival, the word got round that he had been behind that "curtain" and some rather unpleasant reports appeared in the local press.

Another visitor was Ossia Trilling, Wulf's brother-in-law. Among his other activities, Ossia wrote reviews of operas for *The Times* and it was for this purpose that he came to the GDR. Actually he played a little trick on me. The 'phone rang and when I answered, someone spoke to me in fluent German for quite some time and it wasn't until we were well through the conversation that I recognised his voice! My tea-making activities were again in demand. It so happened that Alan was there at the same time and I was able to introduce them, much to Ossia's delight.

I should mention, here, that one of my contacts in England was Denis Hayes, who ran the Leipzig Fair Office in London. As the fair took place twice a year I saw quite a lot of Denis and we became good friends. At which point it is appropriate, perhaps, to explain that the fair was an excellent opportunity for East and West to meet peacefully for commercial purposes and, as far as the GDR was concerned, this was an occasion on which they could stress their policy of peaceful co-existence. It also meant that they were able to acquire a supply of hard currency, the shortage of which greatly hampered their economic development.

There was always great excitement during the fair. At no other time were there so many Westerners around, so many Western cars, for example. From my students' point of view, it was a great opportunity to practice their linguistic skills. Indeed, students were used as interpreters, even before they had finished their courses, rather like school practice for teacher trainees. They were also used for this purpose during international conferences, many of which were held in Leipzig because of the abundance of interpreting skills available.

On one memorable occasion, the Dean of Canterbury visited Leipzig with his wife. I was requested to entertain him and we had a meal together in the Astoria Hotel, just near the station. I had often been an enthusiastic member of the audiences he had addressed and I had read his Left Book Club book: *The Socialist Sixth of the World* but it was my first personal encounter with the "Red Dean". I remember his great delight that snails were on the menu and he ate them with relish. I also noticed that his wife, who was considerably younger than him, was very solicitous and protective of her husband in a number of small ways. I enjoyed the conversation with both of them but the best was yet to come. About a dozen clergymen had been invited to meet him and ply him with questions.

Although there was an official interpreter provided, I was also included, to make him feel at home, I thought, but also to add my two-pennyworth whenever I felt that there was a slight misunderstanding of his meaning. Even the best interpreters can slip up over a nuance here and there. Many and varied were the questions he fielded but, funnily enough, the one I remember best was about his position in the English church. How come the authorities allowed him to retain his high position when he was espousing views that must have been anathema to them? His reply was twofold. Firstly, he claimed that his views were consistent with Christ's sermon, (quoted in Matthew 25 Verse 40), "Inasmuch as ye have done it unto one of the least of these my brethren, ye have done it unto me". Secondly, he told them that he had security of tenure and could only be sacked for immorality and "I'm in love with my wife, so there's no temptation!"

Several progressive American writers came to visit Ebs, whilst I was there. Philip Bonosky, author of *The Magic Fern*, gave me a signed copy of the book that had made him famous But the American writer whom I remember most vividly was Albert Maltz. He was actually a playwright and Hollywood scriptwriter, famed for his plays about working-class life and one of the Hollywood Ten, persecuted during the McCarthy reign of terror. He came to Leipzig with his wife. Ebs was his literary agent and translator in the GDR and when he entertained him in his flat, in the family circle, I was invited too. Mrs. Maltz became a great favourite with the children.

Albert Malz(centre) and his wife (with flowers) on the steps of the English Institute, with Prof. Martin (foreground) Ebs, Albrecht and other colleagues and students.

A change is as good as a rest, they say, so apart from my regular visits back home, before I got married, I had two European holidays whilst domiciled in the GDR. The first was to Golden Sands, a Black Sea resort in Bulgaria. It should be remembered that GDR currency was valueless outside the country, indeed, it was illegal to "export" it, but there were package holidays to other east European countries. This holiday was memorable not only for the wonderful climate and sea swimming that it afforded but also because it led to my meeting a Berlin couple, Herr and Frau Weiss, with whom I became great friends.

Their names were Wolfgang and Dagmar but they invited me to call them Wofuss and Daggi and made me promise that, whenever I visited Berlin, I would stay with them. Our friendship lasted throughout my stay in the GDR and beyond and I had many an enjoyable weekend in their flat in Johannisthal. They had a teenage son who was able to come back home with me on one occasion and meet my parents and sisters.

Wofuss had been an active anti-Nazi pre-war and had frequently been in danger of arrest - and worse. His training as a lawyer meant that the Movement used him to defend their members in court, which was sometimes possible under the Nazis. He later gave me a book, his account of his defence of a Jewish anti-Nazi, tragically unsuccessful in the end. It contains excerpts from this man's diary at the time and he called it *Vom Tagebuch bis zum Todesurteil* (From Diary to Death Sentence).

He was a patron of the *Schiffbauerdamm*, a theatre devoted to the works of Bertholt Brecht, the world-famous communist playwright and poet, where the Berliner Ensemble, a repertory company founded by Brecht, gave regular performances. I went there often, sometimes with Wofuss and on one occasion he introduced me to Helene Weigel, Brecht's widow and a leading actress at the theatre. Her performance as Mother Courage seems to be a benchmark for all other actresses who play that part. As the Brechts lived in America during the war, her English was fluent though, naturally, americanised. We had an animated and enlightening conversation. She was particularly interested in my membership of Unity Theatre, which had performed many Brecht pieces.

Herr and Frau Weiss entertained many foreign and West German visitors, especially artists of various professions. Wanda Wilkomirska, the Polish violinist, always stayed with them when she was performing in Berlin and I met her at their flat. We became very friendly and she invited me to come to Warsaw and stay with her and her husband. As GDR marks were not viable outside the country, she said they would cover my expenses. It

70

was an offer I couldn't refuse. I stayed with them for two weeks and absorbed the Polish capital's historical and cultural treasures.

They also introduced me to their friends: painters, musicians, playwrights and actors. I attended a performance, in Polish, of a play by one of their friends called, *The Devil and Mr.God*. I also went with Wanda and her husband, Mietislav Rakovsky (later to become a leading figure in the government) to the State Yiddish Theatre and was able to assist their understanding of the words from my own meagre knowledge of Yiddish!

Wofuss at that time was director of the GDR travel agency and he arranged an individual tour of the Soviet Union for me. It was expensive but - what else could I do with the GDR money I had accumulated? The three weeks were split between Moscow (ten days), Leningrad (four days) and Yalta, on the Black Sea, (a week). It was my first and last visit to the SU. I do not speak Russian, other then a few words and phrases, but I learnt the alphabet so that I could at least make out the words, many of which are based on Latin or Greek, like many English words, or are international, so I was able to understand quite a bit on posters, shop fronts etc. Additionally, I had an interpreter for some of the time.

The visit was most enjoyable, especially swimming in the sea at Yalta where, incidentally, I was able to visit the palace where the four wartime leaders of the anti-Hitler coalition signed the famous agreement. Apart from that, there were the usual visits to various showpieces and one Moscow factory, where the director was a woman. They were manufacturing pre-fabricated parts for building. Through the interpreter, I spoke to one young girl who was filling a section with padding of some sort. She was studying building construction at evening school. I asked her what her ambition was. She aimed to become director, one day, she said. When I expressed some surprise at this flight of fancy, she pointed out that the present director was a woman. "There's nothing to stop me if I get the necessary qualifications," she said.

It is worth mentioning that Wofuss eventually entered the GDR film world, becoming Director of their Synchronisation, ie film-dubbing Studio. Perhaps as a result of this, he co-produced a film called: *So Macht Man Kanzler* (That's How Chancellors are Made) comparing the careers of Hitler and Adenauer. I still have the beautifully produced book of the film, complete with stills and photographs of the documents cited. In his dedication Wofuss suggested that I might, perhaps, produce and publish an English translation. Sad to say, this never materialised.

Back in Leipzig, there were many visiting professors and lecturers living in my hostel. They came from Poland, the Soviet Union, Rumania and China. I had many an interesting and enlightening chat with them. It was fascinating to observe their different characteristics, to some extent mirroring the culture from which they came. It all added to my international awareness.

As you will have noted, I really had a very extensive social and cultural life, which neatly dovetailed into my professional duties. The intellectual effort required to keep my students, the young and not so young, on their toes was never a burden, despite my own lack of academic training. Indeed, I benefited greatly myself from the work I was pursuing. In many ways my experiences may be regarded as a great human experiment, in which social and professional concerns intermingled and produced some fascinating and certainly beneficial results for "the subject" of the experiment.

ROMANCE

Perhaps this is the chapter the reader has been waiting for. The emotions play an impressive part in our lives. My own experience of marriage had not been a happy one and for many years I was determined to avoid a repeat at all costs. But as the memory of that unhappy experience gradually faded and I found myself in this very strange situation, with all its inhibiting influences and all its temptations, I felt that anything could happen - and it did.

The English Institute had its share of pretty girls, of course, but the Interpreters' Institute was particularly blessed with rather more than its fair share. They came in all sorts of shapes and sizes, some petite and delectable, others of the Valkyrie type, still others tall, slender and alluring. There were blonde bombshells, ravishing raven-hairs and beautiful brunettes. I came there to teach English, of course, but...........! As a long-time divorced bachelor, I was in need of female company. Now whilst the students were not absolutely taboo, there were certain inhibiting factors governing the behaviour of academic staff. One: I was a lecturer, two: I was a foreigner and three: I came from the West, not an unimportant consideration in the GDR.

But things began to look up when, in the spring of 1959, I was put in charge of the English section of the translating room at an international conference in the *Kongresshalle* in Leipzig, a building backing on to the famous Leipzig Zoo and used for concerts as well as meetings. My job was to check the speech translations done by my students and, where necessary, edit - or anglicise - them. These were the texts of speeches provided for us by the speakers beforehand. The translations were then handed on to the simultaneous interpreters who sat closeted in cabins and these pre-translations greatly eased their work.

During pauses in our labours, there was, naturally, a more relaxed atmosphere in which students and supervisors could mix socially. There was much good-humoured chit-chat and not a little flirting, enjoyed by all. And in intervals and meal-times it was possible to wander through the zoo which we did in small groups (or in ones and twos). I walked round with two students who had struck up a friendship, Rita and Hedda. Hedda was bubbly and talkative whilst Rita, an attractive brunette, was somewhat on the shy side.

Rita, snapped on a train journey
1961

When we got to the hippo compound, I sang them the song about "the
hip-hip-hippopotamus" who could "do more than the lot of us". Fortunately
they didn't know the tune - so I was safe! We passed a pleasant hour or so,
getting to know each other. Rita had attracted me quite early on. She didn't set
out to impress, like some of the other girls; I thought I perceived a certain innocence
but a certain inner strength too, which I found immensely appealing. And when,
at the end of the conference, an entertainment was put on followed by a dance in
a hall at the chemical works at Leuna, I made sure that she was aware of my
feelings. We sat out some of the dances, having a drink in the small adjoining
canteen and began to draw closer together.

On the coach home everyone was merry, noisy and full of beans. Rita
and I sat together and communed silently. When we arrived back in Leipzig, one
of the senior interpreters suggested that he and I and the two girls should continue
the evening in a local nightspot, the Regina Bar. There, we danced the night
away until it was time to go home. My home was quite near but Rita lived some
distance away and I insisted on escorting her there on the tram. At the door to
her residence we gave each other a peck on the cheek and she disappeared.
My romance had begun.

Now, as I have indicated, too close a relationship between GDR citizens
and western foreigners was looked on with some suspicion, if not hostility, by the
authorities, so we did not exactly broadcast our affair, once it got going. On the

other hand, we did not take exaggerated precautions, either, and no doubt the security organs were aware of it but, surprisingly, none of our immediate colleagues or friends, except Hedda seemed to know. And that suited us fine. The elderly ladies who "did" for me at HdW got to know her quite well. It was at HdW that I introduced her to the delights of real English tea - with milk - and to toast, and marmalade (brought back from England as it was not even known in the GDR and hardly in West Germany either). She became addicted to these delicacies, as did some of my colleagues, too.

On our first date we went back again to the Regina Bar, where we had a few drinks and danced, among a jolly crowd of revellers. I don't think we ever went there again as our tastes were more for theatre, opera and orchestral concerts, all of which were well catered for in Leipzig. I think I saw more Shakespeare (in German, of course) in the GDR than I had ever done in England and I certainly listened to more music there than at home. I had been to opera in England and thought I knew quite a few of the popular ones, but through Rita, I really got to know the wider world of opera, as she was a very keen opera-goer and had a vastly greater knowledge of it than I had.

Whilst I was there, the new opera house was built, on the same lines, though slightly modified and modernised, as the original house, destroyed during the war. And this was a noticeable feature of the GDR. They invested a surprisingly high proportion of their very limited resources in cultural pursuits, whilst at the same time trying to cope with their housing and other accommodation problems. The human spirit, they insisted, requires more than material sustenance. Haven't we heard that somewhere before, in a somewhat less secular context?

The New Opera House, beflagged on a festive occasion.

75

They had also built the *Deutsche Hochschule für Körperkultur,* (The German College of Physical Culture) which I mentioned briefly, above. This was a whole complex of buildings, a little townlet, so to speak, to promote and train their athletes and gymnasts to compete on the world stage. After I had left, they also built a magnificent new home for the world famous *Gewandhaus* orchestra, right opposite the opera house. I should stress that, at the same time, they were straining to re-house the whole population in new or re-furbished accommodation.

Rita and I also enjoyed long walks in the parks and other open spaces in the city as well as further afield. She came from a beautiful mountainous area up the Elbe, the place where my young friend had done his mountaineering, and was a great lover of nature. We had many a long discussion - and occasionally argument - on practical and ideological, political and philosophical questions. She was critical of some aspects of life in the GDR. I, as a somewhat privileged outsider, was apt to defend the achievements and had sympathy for the difficulties faced by the government of her country (the GDR, not "Germany") whilst she and her family often experienced the harsher realities of life there. And, for a number of reasons, the standard of living and the quality of consumer goods, was, in general, appreciably below that of West Germany, where many GDR citizens had either relatives or other contacts.

I had only been in the GDR about a year when I received a frightening 'phone call from my brother-in-law, Reuben, to the effect that my father had had a heart attack and lay, critically ill, in hospital. I hastily obtained leave of absence from the university and hurried home. I found, to my great relief, that he was already on the mend and the immediate crisis was over. I had hired a car, as I often did on my visits home, so I was able to collect him from hospital. But, of course, it meant that he couldn't go on working.

It may surprise the reader to learn that, at 74, he had still been putting in a full day's work. In fact, it was whilst waiting at a bus-stop to come home that he had first felt the chest pains. He was worried, now, about managing without me. It wasn't just that he felt their letting of rooms and their all too small pensions would be insufficient to keep them going and that my contribution was needed to add my share to the family income. It was also a question of the whole responsibility for the house falling on his now somewhat frailer shoulders.

For reasons that must be clear, I was quite determined to stay in the GDR for quite a while yet! After my one-year's leave of absence was up, I had contacted my employers, the LCC, and persuaded them to give me another two years unpaid leave. After that, they said, they would have to offer my post to someone else. For their part, the university were delighted that I wanted to stay on and very willing to extend my contract.

At the end of the three years, i.e. in 1961, I was still far too involved both in my work as well as in my personal affairs, to contemplate leaving, so I had contacted my Headmaster and he had assured me that, as soon as I wanted to return, he would see to it that there was a position for me in the school. Strangely enough, it was not long after, when my friend, George Rudé, obtained the chair in History at an Australian university and thus left his position as head of department at Holloway School vacant. The Head wrote to me and told me that they had interviewed short-listed candidates twice and, not having found a suitable person, the governors had authorised him to write to me and "suggest that I applied," virtually offering me the job. I turned down even that tempting offer.

But that lay in the future. Meanwhile my father's heart attack gave rise to the financial situation I have described. So I offered to let my parents have half the small part of my salary that was paid in Sterling, which would amount to £10 a month, roughly £80 - £100 at today's values. They accepted this, though reluctantly and, glad that my father was now back to reasonable good health, I returned once again to the place where my heart was.

I don't think we had actually spoken of marriage but my intentions were becoming clear and so what was also becoming clear was that Rita would have to make a decision. She had already turned down a wonderful opportunity to work for a year as an interpreter with the official GDR trade representation in Indonesia, because it involved cutting off any close relationship with a foreigner. I was greatly relieved and my hopes were high when she told me of this. It was indeed a considerable sacrifice of career opportunities that would have stemmed from this prestigious appointment. By turning it down she had left her options open but had still not committed herself to marriage.

When she finished her studies she went to work in Berlin with no decision yet made. On my return from my visit home I found a lovely little framed picture and a note from her on my couch. The picture was of geese in a pond - I still have it and prize it - and the note suggested, without actually saying so, that it was a goodbye present! However, I was sure this was not the final word and, as I had her address in Berlin, though no 'phone number, the next time I stayed with the Weiss's I sent her a telegram, asking her to 'phone me.

Within a remarkably short space of time, the 'phone rang and - need I say more? Our romance began all over again. On another occasion, I again had a feeling of rejection and sent her a somewhat recriminatory note, though carefully couched so as not to offend. The next time we met I felt that she had come to the conclusion that, in the words of the old Thirties pop song: "We just couldn't say goodbye." Soon afterwards we decided to go on holiday together in Mamaia, on the Rumanian Black Sea coast. It was the summer of 1962. The weather was glorious, the hotel accommodation and catering first class and, even more important, we found that we could still stand the sight of each other after two weeks of constant companionship. Our fate was sealed.

Soon after our return, Rita told her parents, for the first time, about our relationship and our decision to get married. They must have wondered who this foreigner was. Had he, perhaps, a wife in England? Was he a suitable match for their only daughter? Worst of all: would he take her home to England, where they could not follow? To calm their fears, she invited them to Leipzig to meet me and judge for themselves. The place where we were to meet was not far from HdW and, as I hurried across the large open square in that direction (late, as usual), I met Rita hurrying to meet me. Her parents were there - and waiting. It was a large restaurant with a dance floor and we had often eaten there before.

I don't know what their first impressions of me were, but I was certainly favourably impressed with them. Her mother had obviously been a beauty in her youth and was still a good-looking woman, with Rita's wide forehead and wide-set eyes. Her father was handsome, tall and erect, with rather penetrating brown eyes and, as I discovered later, a sense of humour to match my own. I may not have immediately dispelled all their doubts but the atmosphere became warmer as we got to know each other and I had a dance with her mother. They realised that Rita's mind was made up and they invited me to their home for Christmas.

They lived in a beautiful area of eastern Germany - central Germany pre-war - which I have already mentioned as a happy hunting ground for mountaineers. Its romantic name, given to it by a nineteenth-century English traveller, was *Sächsische Schweiz* (Saxon Switzerland). Their little village, situated on both sides of the Elbe and claimed by the inhabitants as a *Kurort* (spa), although it has no curative waters, is called Kurort Rathen. It lies at the foot of a mountainous rock, the *Bastei*, which is part of a whole range of sandstone mountains, stretching almost from Dresden right through to Czechoslovakia, as it was then called.

Saxon Switzerland

The Bastei showing bridge leading to viewpoint.

A daring leap

General view of the sandstone mountains

The visit went very well. They treated me like an honoured guest and we had many a cheerful chat over a glass of wine. Her father questioned me, rather fearfully I felt, about how long I planned to stay in the GDR. I told him I had no immediate plans to leave and this seemed to satisfy him. I also told him about my parents and sisters and something of my life in England. He struck me as a decent, upright sort of man, both as to physical stature and character. We were necessarily rather cautious in any tentative political discourse, but I discovered that, although he had not been part of any anti-nazi resistance, his family was staunchly Social-Democrat and he had left a steady job in the police when the authorities insisted on all policemen joining the Nazi Party. He was a man of firm principles and he had some principled criticisms of the GDR.

The wedding was fixed for March 9th 1963, but very few of our friends in the GDR were to hear of the event until the last moment. It really is remarkable how none of them twigged what was going on. The two friends of Rita's who knew, Hedda and another student, must have kept their lips tightly buttoned. And very grateful we were, too. I had informed my family, of course, and urged my parents to make the effort and fly over for the ceremony and to get to know their prospective in-laws.

My father, who was terrified of flying, resolutely set his face against the project but my mother, also very nervous at the prospect of leaving terra firma, was nonetheless determined to see her new daughter-in-law and to see her son wed. It was no accident that the wedding coincided with the Leipzig Fair, as we deemed it expedient to enter mother as an exhibitor in order to expedite the issue of a visa. One amusing result of this was that, for many months afterwards, she received communications from the Fair Office, addressed to Mrs. J. Goldman and Son!

I went home to fetch her; she survived the flight admirably and we were greeted by Rita at the airport. I think they were both favourably impressed. A couple of days before the wedding, we had sent out notices to our friends with a simple message: first in German: *Wir haben es gewagt!* (literally: We have dared (to do) it), of which my very free translation was: We've taken the plunge! Lothar Römer promptly dubbed this: the plunge notice. One problem was that March 8th is International Women's Day, when all women in the GDR received flowers from their male colleagues, so that flowers were terribly difficult to obtain. However, through the good offices of my friend Karl, we managed to get a lovely bunch of white carnations.

We walked arm-in-arm to the registry office, followed by Rita's parents and my mother. Once inside, we were soothed by suitable music and the ceremony was simple and fairly short. I paid eight marks (including 3 marks for the music) and the deed was done. It was the best eight marks I have ever spent in my life. I wore a dark grey suit, purchased in a famous men's shop in Regent St. (still almost new but miles too loose for me now). Rita was in a lovely mauve lace dress, hand-made by a Berlin dressmaker. It still fits her! After the ceremony, Rita's father turned to me, shook hands and said: "We are now Werner and Gretel to you, Len, and you must use the familiar form (of German) with us", an indication that I was now part of the family.

Wedding photo 1963

On our return to my room at HdW, we were overwhelmed by the sight and scent of the huge bunches and vases of flowers that filled the room. Our colleagues - mine in Leipzig and Rita's in Berlin - had done us proud. Even the staff of HdW had added their contribution. It was a delightful surprise. Rita's father took all five of us to lunch at the Hotel International, a favourite haunt of ours and once the venue for the international chess championships, the year when all the fuss was made about the USA refusing to allow Bobby Fisher to attend. When the waiter heard who we were and realised that I was English, he brought two little flags, one of the GDR and the other the Union Jack and they stood on the table, crossed in friendship, for the whole of the meal.

The problem of communication between my mother and Rita's parents was solved that evening, when we all attended a performance of Wagner's *Die Meistersinger* at the magnificent new opera house. Music as an international language once again demonstrated its power. The opera went on for five hours but when I suggested to my eighty-year-old mother that, if she were tired, I'd take her back to the lodgings, she wouldn't hear of it.

One amusing incident was when a singer used a German word which my mother recognised because it was the same in Yiddish, her mother tongue, and she turned to me in great surprise and exclaimed: "He said *verdrossen!*" On another occasion, this linguistic similarity proved rather embarrassing. We were sitting in a restaurant when two large ladies at our table ordered double portions. My mother said to me, in English, "Some people are such greedy eaters!" For the last two words she used the Yiddish word, *fressers,* apparently not realising that it is roughly the same pejorative expression in German!

During her visit, my mother met Ebs's wife, Usch, and an immediate sympathetic bond developed between them, as there did when she met Elfriede, Martin Richter's wife. We saw her off at the airport and settled down to a split-site marriage. Why spilt-site and why no immediate honeymoon? Firstly, Rita had to return to her job in Berlin until she could find another post in Leipzig. But there was also the question of the course she was taking in Portuguese and which she wanted to complete in order to obtain the certificate, a useful addition to her linguistic qualifications. Lastly, it would have been extremely awkward for either of our employers to allow us another break so soon after my holiday in England. The honeymoon simply had to be postponed.

As there was no possibility of my transferring to Berlin, I went on with my work in Leipzig, so we only got together at weekends. Of course, we had no intention of allowing this to continue and Rita set about obtaining a post in Leipzig. However, before this could be arranged, an important change took place in my situation - I bought a car! This was not so easy as it sounds. In the GDR cars were in very short supply and, by comparison with West Germany, very dear.

However, my trade union backed my application (yes, you had to "apply" for one) on the perfectly valid grounds that I needed one for my work, which now involved a certain amount of travelling. I had ordered it in Berlin, for various reasons, and took the train down to pick it up. From the showroom, I drove to Rita's workplace and amazed her, when she emerged, as I had kept the whole project dark. The car was a red Škoda and, despite the many derogatory remarks made about them in England (negative stereotyping by their competitors?) it gave me largely trouble-free motoring for many years, including at least three years in England,

Eventually, Rita got a job as technical translator in the Institute of Tropical and Subtropical Agriculture, in Leipzig and we were able to move into a university-owned flat in the west of the city. But first, the delayed honeymoon. We booked rooms on the Baltic coast and journeyed up there in the Škoda. It was a wonderful time for both of us, swimming in the sea, sunbathing in the little beach shelters, thrilled with each other's company and the time and leisure to enjoy it without pressures and deadlines. On the way home we called at Rita's Berlin flat, loaded all her possessions into the car and made tracks for *Haus der Wissenschaftler* where we stayed until we could move into a flat. Rita had to store her clothes in the attic as there was no space in my small bed-sit.

Rita as interpreter with an African delegation 1962.

83

As the new flat was unfurnished we went on a buying spree and were soon well furnished, some of it to our own design, and well equipped. Rita's parents gave us a magnificent three-compartment wardrobe. When we finally left the GDR we took most of these things with us (including the Škoda) and, thirty-six years later, many of them *still grace our Brighton home*. The flat was in the kind of building known as an "old-new building", a solid structure, with rooms of reasonable size but it had one big disadvantage, there was a plague of flies which seemed to congregate in a large bush just behind the block. And no matter what was tried, nothing cleared them.

After much searching we discovered that a housing co-operative was constructing modern blocks of flats in the southern part of the city, quite near a lovely park. The idea was that, under the guidance of professional builders, all members should take some part in the actual building work. I was accepted into their ranks and we all set to. I shall skip the details and difficulties and simply say that when the project was finished we had an excellent third-floor flat, with one large sitting/dining room, a bedroom, and a modern kitchen and bathroom.

When I tell you that the rent of 80 marks (about £27 at today's rates) per month was regarded as high by most Leipzigers, it will give some idea of how low rents were, in general. Utilities were cheap, too. Our new furniture fitted in nicely, we bought new carpeting and a few more items, especially pictures and were entertaining almost before the last removal man had disappeared down the stairs. Our friends were amazed. Rita's organisational and housekeeping skills, never required before, were beginning to develop and augured well for the future.

And, what was at the time perhaps even more important, we soon became an integrated "couple", accepted as such by our whole circle of friends and acquaintances. It was no longer just Len that they looked to for companionship and stimulus but "Len and Rita". There was only one tiny rift in our relationship, when Rita quite reasonably wanted to continue with our very necessary household shopping well into the afternoon when she had finished work, I wanted nothing more than to pick up some delightful Saxon patisserie, head for home and my own brewed real tea. I think I won, more often than not - she's an indulgent wife.

Many wiseacres in Leipzig and elsewhere were no doubt convinced that our marriage could not be successful. The difference in age, background, nationality, made such a liaison prone to every kind of wreckage but, as all my friends know, these doomsayers have been proved spectacularly wrong. We've not only stuck together for nealy forty years, our partnership has become indissoluble and the depth of our enjoyment of each other is beyond words.

Rita's family home in Rathen.
This house was built by her great grandfather.

THE YOUNG ELIZABETHANS

One important milestone in my activities in the GDR was the visit of a youth theatre group to Weimar, which I organised on the occasion of the Shakespeare quater-centenary celebrations, in 1964, which were enthusiastically carried out in the GDR, as elsewhere in the world, on the four-hundredth anniversary of Shakespeare's birth. Weimar was the seat of the German-Shakespeare Society which, exceptionally, included West German participants!. The idea was sold to me by Charles Green, my old colleague and friend from Acland School. He was in touch with a teacher, Bobby Brown, who had organised an amateur drama group called The Young Elizabethans, who'd had some considerable success in London with their production of Shakespearean plays. They had also performed at the Edinburgh Festival and even, on one memorable occasion, in Hamburg.

On my return to London, Charles introduced me to Bobby, who was also their producer, and suggested to me that it would be a good idea if the GDR were to invite these young people to the celebrations, to put on their acclaimed performance of *Hamlet*. It seemed to me at the time a rather tall order, sensing the bureaucratic obstacles that would be in the way and thinking that the GDR would hardly be likely to undertake the considerable expense involved for what was, after all, an amateur group of unknown potential. However, I agreed to give it a go and, on my return to Leipzig, set about the daunting task of promoting the visit.

I explained the plan to Rita, who was now a professional interpreter, and she agreed to help. First, I asked for and, what is more astounding got, an interview with the Minister of Culture. On entering his office, I was met by his secretary, a very beautiful young woman, superbly groomed and smooth in the extreme. She was very friendly, smiled a lot and asked me to wait a moment for the minister. When he arrived I took him in at a glance. Small of stature, he had a large head, surmounted by handsomely coiffured grey hair. Every hair was in place, as though it had been painted on. He was full of confidence and bonhomie.

He turned out to be most amenable and, as my German was quite fluent by this time, we had a detailed discussion and it was agreed that the GDR would not only invite the youth group but, what was more important, pay all the expenses, including the air fare. He seemed to see the whole scheme as an excellent example of co-operation between the two countries, though quite unofficial on my part, of course. But this didn't seem to matter. I was delighted, walking on air, in fact. To this day I don't know why the authorities were prepared to fall in with my plan but they did, and that was all that mattered.

The Minister of Culture (L) and his wife greet young 'Hamlet'

On my next trip home, I finalised the arrangement at that end and, on returning, awaited the arrival of the Young Elizabethans. I wasn't there to meet them, as they arrived in the early hours, after considerable delays - and without a very important part of their baggage, namely, their costumes! However, when I sought them out in their very commodious lodgings, they were in excellent spirits. As it turned out, the National Theatre in Weimar, hearing of their predicament, had agreed to lend them a complete set of costumes for *Hamlet*.

The celebrations were extensive, however I shall not go into them here but concentrate on the little group of youngsters whom I had managed to bring over. For them, of course, it was a very exciting adventure. Most of them were thoroughly indoctrinated with Cold War propaganda about the "Iron Curtain countries" and were prepared, on the one hand, to be propagandised and, on the other, to suffer the privations which GDR citizens were supposed to be undergoing. And although both these forebodings proved false, there's no easy overturning of prejudice. The best example of this was a comment made to me by Beryl Piesse, the girl who played Ophelia, after a broadcast speech by Walter Ulbricht, the GDR leader at the time. He devoted his remarks to the importance of Shakespeare as a great humanist. Beryl had an elementary acquaintanceship with German and she remarked to me, "As soon as I heard him describe Shakespeare as a communist, I switched off"!

The Shakespeare memorial in Weimar. I'm caught looking up at the great man. 1964.

Some of the actors preparing for their TV interview. Bobby Brown, producer (centre), Dr Walch, interpreter (seated on the ground).

The group were assigned a delightful little theatre belonging to Schloss Belvedere, situated in lovely parkland where Goethe's small house still stands. Their performance was a great success and they were interviewed on television. After the premiere, the minister, who had personally attended, took me aside and told me, in confidential tones, "One should not underestimate the importance of this for our whole celebrations." After another performance, I noticed a very distinguished man during the interval whom I was sure I knew. It eventually dawned on me that it was André van Gysegham, a British actor who had produced the first play I was in at Unity Theatre, before the war. He had recognised me, too, but couldn't remember my name, so had asked one of my colleagues. Thus he was able to come to me and say, "Hallo, Len. Long time no see." After the show, we reminisced into the early hours.

One of the very pleasant features of the celebrations was the reception that was held. This was quite a lavish affair attended by the GDR top brass. Several ministers and Ulbricht, himself, were there. We were all invited and eventually a minion approached me and indicated that the great man would like words with Charles Green and me. There didn't seem to be an official interpreter so Rita and I were able to help here and there. He asked Charles what he thought of Weimar and Charles was full of praise for the wonderful, historical buildings. This wasn't quite what Ulbricht had in mind. He was referring to the rebuilding which had gone on.

Charles was a little more doubtful about this but Ulbricht claimed that they had tried, within their limited resources, to fit in with the older buildings. It was chit-chat, really, but enabled us to get a closer and more personal look at the leader of the GDR. I would only add that my wife and I were fully recompensed for our expenses and also for the interpreting and organising activities which we had undertaken. Altogether a thoroughly worthwhile enterprise, I reckoned.

And so, apparently, did Bobby Brown, who wrote to me afterwards. "I think that our ten days," he wrote, "represent just about the most exhilarating time I've known. I can't thank you enough for your perpetual care for us and for the stimulus you have provided. The effects of the trip upon all my youngsters (and "oldsters") has been quite staggering. It has given them a real opportunity to reassess some of their ideas which, as you know, only too readily solidify too early and stay that way for a lifetime." He also thanked

Rita in glowing terms. Indeed, the successful outcome of the whole enterprise would have been quite unthinkable without her considerable input, both as interpreter and organiser.

The Young Elizabethans were not the only British entertainers to give public performances in the GDR. Two acquaintances of mine in England were members of a large progressive movement of folk singers, of whom the most famous was Ewan MacColl. Their names were Betty and Fred Dallas and they sang songs of peace as well as those that highlighted social problems. Having toured West Germany, they had organised a singing trip to the GDR and I was glad to help in any way I could. When they came to Leipzig, I got them to do a show at *Haus der Wissenschaftler* and invited a number of colleagues along.

All the staff on duty at the time were also in the audience. They put in an appearance at the local cinema too, a hastily arranged concert that I persuaded the cinema management to allow. Their concert was a tour de force that brought the house down. Fred had a few words of German and used them to great effect. The audience took to his nonchalant style and he and they thoroughly enjoyed the experience.

Fred and Betty Dallas in performance in West Germany.

"Men and women stand together,
Do not heed the the men of war;
Make your mind up, now or never;
Ban the bomb for evermore!"

GOODBYE RATHEN - GOODBYE GDR

Now that we were married, Werner and Gretel (*Vati* and *Mutti* to Rita) wanted to see us as often as possible and we were keen to see them and enjoy the wonderful scenery of Rita's home area and the wonderful hospitality her parents offered. It was a large, detached house in the main village street, built by Werner's grandparents as a holiday bed-and-breakfast accommodation, with several rooms on each of the three storeys and two spare rooms in the flat which they occupied, so there was never any shortage of space when we came there.

With Rita and her parents in the mountains

I gradually got to know the whole family: *Tante Rosel* (Auntie Rosie) and her two children (she'd lost her husband during the war), who occupied the family home and *Onkel Kurt* and *Tante Ilse* and their twin daughters, who lived in Dresden. These were all on Gretel's side of the family as Werner was an only child. We used to drive from Leipzig to Rathen through the countryside until we got to Dresden. Having negotiated our way through this large city, we hit the mountains and knew that we were "home".

And what a home it was! The fantastic shapes of these rocky sandstone mountains have to be seen to be believed. They are not very high but, as I have said, they provide excellent climbing opportunities with varying degrees of difficulty. Several well known heights can be seen from Rathen: there is the *Bastei*, which I have already mentioned, towering above the Elbe as it flows through the village, dividing it in two, with the railway station on one side and Rita's house on the other. The next most famous one is the *Lilienstein*, standing out from the plain almost like a flat-topped castle. Werner knew the area like the back of his own hand and could stand there and name all the mountains for miles around. I was taken on many a hike through this glorious countryside. There were easier sides to the mountains where you could walk to the top, though I was pretty puffed out at the end of a day's sojourn; puffed out, pleasantly tired - and happy.

A little relaxation

When I told Werner that I had no immediate plans to return to England, that was perfectly true. I still had a variety of interesting work to do: watching over my students, working out methods of improving their linguistic skills, writing textbooks, giving talks about England and, now that I look back, trying to perfect my German. I had also become very fond of my in-laws. But after a year or two of married life, I decided that it was time to go back. After all, I had parents too - and sisters and many close friends.

The first step was to convince Rita that this would be a good move. And it wasn't easy. As you were constantly told, there were indeed many GDR citizens who wanted to leave for the West, and no doubt a lot of her fellow-students would have jumped at the chance. But Rita was far from keen. Through me and, no doubt, the propaganda of the authorities, she knew that the "golden West" had its less golden side. And then, there were her parents. It would not be easy for them to travel to us and, although we could always go back there, would we be able to afford it? Most of all, perhaps, it meant giving up her secure job - and with it her secure future - and our lovely very inexpensive flat, to face a very uncertain employment and housing situation in Britain, where neither of us had a home or guaranteed employment. On the other hand, she was well aware of the advantages for her personal and professional development that experience in England would bring.

When she finally agreed to the move, we set about getting the necessary permission. This turned out to be somewhat easier than it otherwise might have been because we had previously taken the necessary steps to overcome what would have been a serious obstacle. To obtain permission to enter Britain she needed a visa stamped on her passport. Aye, there was the rub. The GDR was not recognised by any western power and so there was no British Embassy to turn to and, in any case, her GDR Identity Card wasn't recognised, either. The GDR rightly objected very strongly to the West German claim to represent all Germans, by implication, that they were the rightful rulers of all "Germany".

In pursuance of this claim they were prepared to issue "passports" to any GDR citizen who managed - by one means or another - to cross the border. These documents were franked with the words "presumed German"!! Obviously this was neither possible nor desirable for Rita and, in any case, I would not contemplate such a move. What to do? The best way was to obtain British citizenship. But how? We solved this by travelling to Prague and contacting the British representative there. He was very helpful and even cut a few corners so that she could not only get British citizenship but a passport too.

As the GDR allowed double-citizenship, Rita was now in possession of two passports. With her GDR pass, suitably franked with an exit visa, she was able to leave the GDR legally and, of course her British passport ensured her of entry to Britain. It was 1965 and we planned to "emigrate" in the summer but, meanwhile, it seemed a good idea for us to have a short holiday in Britain first. We decided to go in February and, although it was more difficult to get permission for a temporary visit to the West than it would be when we left more permanently, we managed it and alerted my family and friends.

There was a Polish airline (Lot) which flew from Berlin to Heathrow and my friend Peter Borin agreed to pick us up from the airport and drive us home. There's friendship for you! Sure enough, when we emerged from the customs, there were Peter and Bonnie and Jeffrey, their young son, holding an enormous box of chocolates, which he confidently presented to Rita. A sweet beginning indeed, and a first indication of the sort of reception she might expect.

Of course, all my family and friends wanted to take a look at my new bride - new to them, at any rate. I have reason to believe that they were all very happy with what they saw and they certainly made her very welcome. My mother knew her already, of course, and now it was my father's turn and I'm sure he was delighted with his new daughter-in-law. The Borins made her as welcome as they had always made me, as did Nicky and Barrie Amiel and their whole family. Other local friends and comrades followed suit. My oldest friend, Wulf, and his wife, Lulu, were very hospitable too. In short, Rita became a natural and fixed part of my rather large circle, auguring well for her permanent settlement in England.

I was keen for her to see Brighton and visit some of my old haunts. Unfortunately, when we went there, it was a miserable, rainy day and I doubt if she got the impression I was hoping for. The fact is, I had decided that, although my former London Headmaster had promised me a position at Holloway when I returned, I wanted to teach in Brighton, where I had, myself, been to school. It seems that the town in which I grew up and where my early experiences had helped to shape my emotional life, my practical and intellectual skills and therefore my whole outlook, still had an enormous pull on my affections.

Some months earlier, whilst still abroad, I had written to the Chief Education Officer in Brighton, a certain Dr. Stone, enquiring whether there were any teaching vacancies in the town. He had sent a friendly reply, inviting me to visit him when I came home. I duly turned up at his office, only to find that he was on holiday. However, his deputy received me cordially and asked me to go along to Dorothy Stringer School, where he thought there might be at least a temporary vacancy, to replace a colleague on a year's course.

The Deputy Head, Ted Hood, interviewed me and we had a long, friendly chat. It turned out that he knew my old teacher, "Wag" Gordon, had, indeed, played football with him in the Yale club, whose canary-coloured jerseys I remembered so well! That was a good start, anyway, I thought to myself, as Rita and I returned to London, although there was no definite promise of a job. Imagine my surprise then, when a day later, I received a call to come back to Brighton to be presented with the offer of a position at the school. It was to be for a year, to start with but, so the Head assured me, there was a good likelihood of its being extended to a permanency, when the time came. I had a job to return to!

Back in the GDR it was difficult to settle down to the old routine, which had become an accepted part of my life, just as I had become almost a part of the furniture. My colleagues were not at all happy to see me go. They had come to rely on me professionally and my personal relationship with many of them was close and deep. The university gave me an excellent reference, detailing and expressing thanks for the help I had given to staff and students. Before the fond farewells could begin, however, there were the extensive, bureaucratic procedures to work our way through.

Every item of household goods, every picture, every book, every disc, had first to be recorded, *in quintuplicate* and then endorsed by a signature accompanied by an office stamp. And each different category had to be endorsed *by a different office*. Before you rush in with condemnation of GDR bureaucracy, however, let me assure you that these procedures predated the GDR - and even the Hitler period - they dated from the days of the Kaiser and nobody had thought to amend or rescind them! Some of our possessions would be packed into the Škoda and brought with us, as the car was being transported on the ship that was to take us to England. The considerable remainder would be packed - by an authorised packer - into several crates and carried on a separate freighter.

Having taken leave of all Leipzig friends and acquaintances, as well as of those in Berlin, we drove the laden Škoda to Rathen to say goodbye to Rita's parents, relatives and friends. Werner and Gretel were not at all happy at the prospect of "losing" their daughter but we assured them that we would be back fairly soon and frequently thereafter. I think that, by now, they had come to realise that Rita was in good hands and that a loyal husband and his family would take good care of her.

From Rathen, we made our way to the Baltic port of Rostock and boarded the *Theodor Koerner*, bound for Cuba. It would take us to Dagenham, in the Thames estuary, where it was to drop us and pick up a cargo of Leyland buses being exported to Cuba in addition to heavy goods from the GDR. We met many interesting people on board including the Hungarian ambassador to Cuba. Like me, he also had his car with him. It was a Dutch DAF, with a Wankel engine, whose workings he explained to me in some detail. The things you learn on a sea voyage! Because of bad weather, we sailed through the Kiel Canal, instead of the usual route round the coast. Normally, GDR ships did not travel through West German waters.

Rita, the Hungarian ambassador and his wife, on the SS Theodor Koerner.

During the voyage, I learnt that I would not be allowed to drive my car home from Dagenham, as I had intended, as there were some bureaucratic procedures to go through first! Fortunately we were near enough to England for me to use the ship's telephone. I got through to Peter and told him of our plight. He immediately agreed to come and pick us up, as I had hoped. Whilst we were in the harbour and waiting to tie up, I was summoned to the captain's room and found a man from the Foreign Office (I assumed) or maybe from MI5.

He was very polite and "just wanted to ask a few questions". The only one I remember was: "Why did you decide to come back to Britain?" What lay behind the question? Your guess is as good as mine. However, I had the temerity to suggest that he was asking me the wrong question. The real question, I insisted, was: Why did I stay abroad so long, when my original idea was to have a change of scenery for a year? I didn't think it necessary to explain my reasons for wanting to come home. Most ordinary people would have no problem in understanding that. If the FO had difficulty in doing so, that was their problem!

Before leaving the subject, I feel I ought to sum up my impressions of the country that had been my "temporary" home for seven years. To do this adequately would require a book on its own. Was it: "that hell-hole behind the Berlin wall", built to prevent its citizens "escaping to the free West", or was it "a workers' paradise, where no man exploits another and all is for the best in the best of all possible worlds"? You will not be surprised to learn that the truth lies somewhere between those two extremes.

I am well aware that I was a somewhat privileged foreigner and that all my experiences were largely on the "outside". Nevertheless, I think I can claim that my very varied life's experience before I went there, the Khruschev revelations and their effect on my political perceptions, as well as the degree of integration I achieved, through my seven years' residence there, deep and intimate friendships and, above all marriage, qualify me to make more rational judgements than those, especially in the influential media, whose acquaintance with the GDR was, at best fleeting and, at worst, totally second-hand.

Its government claimed legitimate sovereignty over about a quarter of what had been a united country (and even "empire", whether under the Kaiser or under Hitler). It owed its existence to the results of the most destructive war in history and the divisions which arose among the allies of the anti-Hitler coalition. The Cold War had begun and the West decided that their zones should become the Federal Republic of Germany and, six months later, the SU had presided over the establishment of the German Democratic Republic.

That it always had been the poorest part of Germany was not its only problem. Its mentor, the SU, was itself impoverished from a war that had seen its European area twice devastated and which had lost, we now know, some 30 million dead. The USA, on the other hand, had suffered comparatively little loss of life and, instead of being poorer as a result of the war, had actually multiplied its capital goods eight times. That's how capitalism works. As someone once said: "War is terrible - but also terribly profitable!"

So the US could subsidise its political friends, of which West Germany was the most important in Europe, whilst the SU actually demanded reparations from those ruling its part of the former enemy territory. The result was predictable, whatever the results of other circumstances may have been: an "economic miracle" in the West but a painfully slow recovery in the East. So the first obstacle to progress in the East was the loss of some of its most productive workers and professionals trained at great expense, to the more prosperous West, a Merc being more attractive than a Trabant, so to speak. And this relative backwardness was to dog the GDR throughout its whole existence.

One noticed it in the quality and quantity of its consumer products and in its inability, due to a chronic shortage of hard currency, to import articles and foodstuffs taken for granted in Britain and elsewhere Cars were expensive, technically and aesthetically inferior to those in the West and - you usually had to wait years and years to get one. And, perhaps the most heavily felt of all disadvantages, it was virtually impossible to travel to the West unless you had some exceptionally good reason, although this was mitigated for pensioners who could travel to the Federal Republic once a year to see their relatives.

Politically, it was not only beholden to the SU and still occupied by Soviet troops but it was also encumbered by a rigid adherence to a culture of control, *supposedly* based on a Marxist interpretation of social needs. One felt this in all areas of public life. Whilst paying enormous lip-service to public participation in decision-making - "rule with us" was the slogan - the "line" was laid down at the highest levels and any suggested deviation from it, even in furtherance of socialist goals, was regarded at best with suspicion and at worst as downright treason.

This had the double effect of stultifying discussion and depriving the administration of what I call the genius of the people, which is, or should be the very essence of socialism. Thus, in my view, they were cutting the ground from under their own feet and (though I admit this is with hindsight) ensuring the tragic end of their efforts to establish it. I did my best to explain to the students - and all who would listen - the benefits of socialism over capitalism, only to meet very frequently with the disarming reply that they had nothing against socialism and largely agreed with my views but objected to "the way it is being practised here". Which is not to say that there were not many fervent supporters of the regime, who protested that much of the criticism was invalid because it exaggerated the negative and ignored the positive aspects of life in the GDR.

To be fair, the GDR was under a number of constraints: the economic problems I have outlined above; the bitter hostility of the US working through its agent, the Federal Republic, with its handy centre in West Berlin, right at the heart of the GDR, from where they could sabotage its efforts to build a new kind of society; the influence (to put it no stronger) of the SU and the perceived duty of loyalty to the "socialist community of nations".

What were the positive aspects? Well, they were considerable. There was no unemployment. Everyone of working age had the constitutional right to work. Most major industry and commerce was nationalised and, if the management of an enterprise wanted to discharge a worker, they had first to make sure that there was another job he or she could go to. Of course, this advantage for the worker could, from another point of view, be a disadvantage to the economy as a whole

Then there was a completely free-at-the-point-of-need health service, including optical and dental services. Education was entirely free. Crèches and kindergartens were available for all who wanted them, with a small charge for meals. Schooling was in Comprehensive Schools from 6 to 16, when all pupils sat a School Leaving Examination. Then they could go on to something like a Sixth Form College, if their grades for the previous year were good enough, or if, after consultation with the teachers, their parents desired it.

At 18 they sat the *Abitur* in nearly all school subjects, both a qualification in itself and also an entrance to university. Those who left at 16 got an apprenticeship and the possibility of doing an extra year to get their *Abitur* as well, if they wanted to. Just before I left, a new law was introduced to pay all post-16 students an apprentice's wage. I once thought of writing a book on the GDR education system. But I'm afraid that will have to wait.

Maternity leave was for one year on full pay, with the guarantee of the job back if desired and, of course, a place in the firm's crèche for the baby. The prices of all children's requirements were heavily subsidised as were those for cultural pursuits and especially for books. Seats in theatres and opera houses were very cheap by our standards and factories and other workplaces were allocated season tickets for these entertainments. I noted a striking difference between the audiences at, for example, operas there - and here!

Rents were minimal - good for tenants but not so good for landlords who were sometimes unable to afford repairs, fares and public utilities cost little - but getting a telephone was difficult. In the Eighties a great housing programme was under way. Millions of older homes were modernised and new ones built. But the standard of equipment and building materials was below what we are accustomed to. A mixed bag, indeed, but a very different picture from the one painted by the media over here which still, ten years after the end of the Cold War, refers to the GDR as "the former East Germany", still unwilling to grant it, posthumously, national statehood, despite the fact that it was eventually recognised by every country except West Germany, held a seat in the UN, and on all its agencies.

What about the "Stasi", the GDR security organ? Every country has one; its West German counterpart was particularly active. The ubiquitous activities of the "Stasi" were the product of a very real and very valid fear of Western, especially American spying and sabotage activities, carried out via their German ally. That it became so obsessive and eventually self-defeating, can be put down to this same paranoia emanating from the SU and affecting all aspects of life in all the self-styled socialist countries.

I often wondered whether I was under suspicion. No direct attempt was made to recruit me which, if a BBC programme is to be believed, was the fate of other English people who worked in or visited the GDR. But I felt, once or twice, that I was being sounded out. If so, those doing the sounding were left in no doubt of my rejection of any such suggestion. On my visits home and, even more, since my return, I have given many talks to TU branches, Labour Party branches, Co-op guilds, schools and other interested organisations, about the GDR. I have always stressed its negative and positive sides. My conclusion: under the eventually impossible circumstances, they tried to introduce a peaceful and progressive form of socialism, containing many elements of what socialism will look like when we achieve it (as I'm sure we will) but that it failed for two reasons. Firstly, their own serious defects and, secondly, the actions of their enemies, in whose hands history had placed overwhelming power.

BRIGHTON
EARLY YEARS AT DOROTHY STRINGER SCHOOL

It was 33 years since I had last lived in Brighton. I had been back on visits several times but the idea of making my home there again only came to me when, in the GDR, I was considering my return to England. I'd always nursed a kind of nostalgia for the place. It was the nearest thing I had to my "roots"; although the family had only lived there some dozen years, they were the formative years of my life: my schooldays and early working experience and it had always held a certain fascination for me. I thought I might perhaps meet up with my old schoolmaster, Wag Gordon, who had had such a great influence on my thinking and had brought out my latent talent for the English language in all its forms and my attraction for acting and the theatre. Maybe I would meet some of my old school friends, too.

I had "seen the world" and now I wanted a re-acquaintance with old haunts. Perhaps I indulged in sentimental thoughts of recapturing some of the old magic and rekindling some of my old boyhood dreams. Whatever the reasons - here I was, back in my old hometown. The first thing to do, before settling here, was to find somewhere to live. We were staying with my parents in London and travelling down to Brighton, house-hunting. Whilst in Brighton the previous February, I had bumped into an old friend and colleague, Norman Owens, whom I had helped to find accommodation when he was teaching in London. He was now Headmaster of a Junior School in Sussex and lived in Westfield Crescent. I told him of my plans and he suggested I ought to visit them when I came to Brighton.

I took him at his word and, after a pleasant meal with him and his family, he suggested that we could stay in his house when the family went off on their holiday for a fortnight and use the time to find a permanent home. The only condition was that we should look after the cat! Although we fed the cat regularly, we showed little affection for it and, after a few days of this emotional neglect, it departed we knew not whence. The fortnight came to an end and we were packing the car, prior to departure, wondering how to face the vanished cat's owners, when the animal suddenly reappeared. It seemed to know that these non-cat-loving barbarians would soon be gone and its caring owners returning.

Shortly before this, we had visited the Crees. Gordon and Doris were old comrades. I didn't know Gordon but had met Doris when she was on a Co-op delegation to the GDR some years earlier and had invited me to contact them, "when you're down our way". Gordon was an insurance rep for the Co-op insurance company (CIS) and the long-time secretary of Brighton Trades Council. We quickly established a close friendship and, when they heard of our situation and the impending return of the Owens family, they told us that *they* were going on holiday and we could stay in *their* house until they came back or until we got a place of our own. We seemed to be in luck, offered accommodation each time we needed it. They had a dog but this was not our responsibility, as their teenage twins were in the house.

We had not found a property before they came back, so we continued to stay in their very commodious house in Hanover Crescent whilst continuing our search. Indeed, we were still there when we both started work. But we had begun to show an interest in the bungalow opposite the Owens' house in Westfield Crescent and eventually secured it. After redecorating and installing central heating, we found that all our furniture and fittings and even carpets which we had brought from the GDR fitted very nicely into our new abode.

Now I had to start acquainting myself with the school situation in Brighton. When I'd left London, seven years earlier, the LCC had already begun the reform which would create Comprehensive Schools, either from existing Grammar or Modern Secondaries or completely newly built ones. Holloway Comprehensive School, where I had taught before leaving for Germany, had previously been a Grammar School. In Brighton, to my horrified surprise, the whole idea of this reform seemed to be anathema to most of those engaged in education in the town. The term "factory schools", coined by the enemies of Comprehensives, was widely in use.

Norman Carter, the Head, a short, bespectacled man with greying, sandy-coloured hair was from Derbyshire and told me he had once "had the boots on with Dally Duncan" (a famous Derby County footballer). He was reasonably progressive and politically astute enough to realise the way the wind was blowing and, in all the major towns and cities, it was blowing in the Comprehensive direction. But he wasn't prepared to make a stand, especially as the Tory town council was dead against the Comprehensive idea.

Stringer, as we called it, was organised on traditional lines, with strict streaming. So, in addition to having "failed" the Eleven Plus, the bottom streams were written off as "failures" even in the lowly Secondary Modern School! How much bigger a "failure" can you get? Naturally, these were the classes that gave the most trouble. The circumstances that were largely responsible for producing their poor academic standing were social constructs that were not likely to change in a hurry. And whilst no teacher would actually admit publicly that they had abandoned any attempt to raise these pupils' standards and self-esteem, that was the practical reality. And how tempting it was to do so.

The Deputy Head was Ted Hood, a Geordie with a sporting background, who had been a member of a mining family and whose most treasured possession was a miner's lamp, presented to him for services rendered. By the time I arrived, he had long since given up football. In addition to being Deputy, he was also Head of History. Although I had been taken on to deputise for a geography teacher who was on a course, I managed to get some History teaching. But when I asked Ted for the History syllabus he handed me a hand-written sheet of paper with a few generalities on it and that was that. So I devised my own. As he was teaching the 'O' Level class, I presume he used the official syllabus for that examination. It wasn't long, however, before I was offered the Head of History post - but with no extra pay for the extra responsibility! That was due to the LEA's level of funding.

The staff at Dorothy Stringer School. c 1970

I took it on, however, and introduced my own syllabus, based on the one I had used in London. I was now responsible for 'O' level History and decided to choose the Industrial Revolution period and subsequent economic developments up to the Second World War and beyond. My Economics degree, for which I had majored in Economic History, was a significant help in this and one increases one's knowledge by having to teach it over many years. It is important to have a much deeper understanding of the material than is required for the purposes of the exam, so that the pupils can feel that there is weight behind what they are taught. But the important thing is to arouse their interest in the subject sufficiently for them to seek out the details for themselves.

I taught other subjects, too, notably Geography, for which I had originally been engaged, English and Maths. And for one glorious year, much later, the Head was able to give me a German class. The pupils seemed to enjoy it, too, and we even put on a couple of sketches in the language for the general entertainment of the rest of the school. I once also took part, myself, in a staff pantomime, written by a temporary teacher. It was a kind of spoof Aladdin, I think, and I was a geni. I'm told that the Head's wife, who attended one of the performances, nearly fell off her chair in paroxysms of laughter when I appeared in my pyjamas and a lion's-head rug.

I was later asked by the PE teacher if I would take over First Year football, be responsible for training, choosing the school team (sport was very competitive in those days), turning up every Saturday to the match to support and encourage the team, and taking my turn at refereeing.   I undertook this without, perhaps, realising what a time-taking and burdensome task it would be. It was extra, completely unpaid work but we had a lot of fun, although I was never able to match the fierce, almost obsessive partisanship of my opposite numbers from other schools. I found their intensity amusing but even quite frightening at times.

I began to get to know my colleagues and to make friends. Some of these friendships have endured to the present day. One with whom I struck up a friendship was Ruby Besch, the Art mistress, whose husband, Bernard, taught Science at another Brighton school but was also a great singer, a member of the Brighton Festival Chorus. They both had views of education and society similar to my own and this helped to draw us together. That is to say, we saw children as being at a particular stage of their lives and ripe for further development, not as static specimens destined to remain in the state in which we found them and therefore to be labelled as such: "dunce", "bright" and various stages in between, as so many people did - and do - even teachers, who ought to know better.

We believed in the enormous developmental possibilities in each child, which it was the school's task to bring out. This often meant trying to overcome the handicaps that restricted some children like a straitjacket and not to accept the notion that this constraint was irremovable. And this is the core of the educational debate. It is mixed up with theories of intelligence and the power (or lack of it) of outside influences to *change* young human beings. This debate still rages today and lies behind school ethos and inner organisation. The Besches and I believed in that power and that it was essential, as a first step, to convince the children that you had faith in them in order that they should have faith in themselves, absolutely essential in the learning process.

So many children came to school already beaten. Why try, when it was hopeless? So why not at least amuse yourself at the teacher's or anybody else's expense? This attitude was at the root of much of the misbehaviour we had to deal with. There were other reasons, too, of course, often connected with domestic or street situations. Parents were involved as far as possible, parents' evenings and so on were organised. But, as any teacher will tell you, the parents with whom we most wanted to discuss their children often stayed away!

Another colleague I got to know well was Norman Down, a small but very tough and wiry chap who taught Maths but was also a keen sportsman and who had played rugby with a local club until quite recently. He and his very pretty wife and two children, one of them at Varndean, lived round the corner from us. He'd been in the RAF and there was still something of the wartime airman about him. He always had a sort of worried look but it didn't seem to express an inner feeling.

Then there was Erica Stratta, another Left-winger, who was responsible for the "backward" third-year group. It contained some of the problem children and was not easy to handle. Erica was always to be seen lugging a tape-recorder around which she used to create interest and stimulate her reluctant charges. She was successful - up to a point. But she had to battle against the notion that her job was to keep these children out of the hair of the rest of us. Hardly a perception leading to serious education. She was also doing a doctorate (on the education of criminals, no less) at Sussex. Her husband was Head of English at Bernard Besch's school and later landed a university job at Birmingham. They were both, like me, active in the local NUT association and it was there that our mutually shared views led to close collaboration.

Speaking of one's educational approach, I should mention Ian Elliot, Head of Science, because our relationship illustrates an interesting point. Ian and I held opposing views on the Comprehensive question and frequently argued about it. But - and it is an important but - I felt there was a sympathy between us that could bridge any ideological differences. I greatly admired his practical and organisational skills, skills which were eventually rewarded by the Authority with promotion to an all-Brighton post in charge of teaching aids and, later, as the very efficient warden of the Teachers' Centre. His teaching ability was obvious to all. I respected him as a colleague and I like to think that he felt the same way, whatever our differences.

When my year's temporary contract was over, and some time before I took over the History Department, Mr. Carter offered me a permanency if I agreed to take Erica's class. Of course, I accepted. They were now fourth-year pupils, i.e. fifteen years of age and able to leave school at the end of the year, if they wished. And it was assumed that they would wish, that they were only longing for the day. These "early leavers" (not staying on an extra year voluntarily, to take the GCE) were known as the "Newsome Group" - soon to be dubbed the "Nuisance Group"! The name originated from the Newsome Committee's report on early leaving and its recommendation that special provision should be made so that the last year of such pupils' schooling should not be wasted.

I felt that my first task was to assure the class that they were just as valuable to me as any other in the school, and to convince them that they had as much creativity as anyone else and that there would be no excuse for an indifferent attitude to the work. This was delivered to them as a kind of homily but I was well aware that mere words could - and no doubt would - be easily ignored. These children had been impressed, many of them from their earliest school experience, that they were dunces, of little worth and that only by making a nuisance of themselves could they be noticed at all. And, despite Erica's best efforts, most of them still needed convincing that they could make something of their lives.

Some of my Newsome Group

John, a skinny, white-faced youth with whom I think I failed completely, was one of a family of children who had been found, abandoned by their parents, screaming their heads off in a neglected flat. Small wonder that he felt the whole world was against him and so, quite naturally, he was against the whole world. He neatly summed up the attitude of several of the others: "Why do we always have to get do-gooders like Mrs. Stratta and Mr. Goldman, who actually want to teach us something and expect us to *work!*" he complained. The other Newsome Group had a teacher with a very different approach. He got them doing manual work, like moving desks, and "kept them out of mischief" that way. At the end of my first year with this group, I was gratified to receive a lovely thank-you card, signed by the whole group - including John!

I struggled along with these Newsome groups for several years with varying degrees of success - and failure. My basic aim was to convince them that they could achieve quite high standards, especially in English, my main concern. Ability to express themselves and to use their imagination would greatly increase their confidence, lack of which was the mainspring of their determination not even to try to comply with school demands and, on the contrary, to make as big a nuisance of themselves as they could get away with. The "Nuisance group" indeed.

Here again I found the "viewpoint" method (referred to above) very effective. Perhaps it might be of interest to quote from some of the efforts of these "hopeless" pupils, once they had grasped the idea. It was my great delight, on the occasions of Year assemblies, to read some of these out to the whole Fourth Year, including the top achievers, who only too willingly accepted the general view of the "Newsome kids". I deliberately picked the work of pupils with the worst reputations and - also deliberately - didn't give their name until the level of achievement had sunk in: and then only with the author's permission, such children being often very sensitive.

There was the boy with a semi-criminal background who felt it his duty to amuse the rest of the class at the teacher's expense - if he could get away with it. Creative writing? Forget it! But he wrote, in an essay on The Fog: " ..the dampness wrapping itself round me like a blanket.." "..alien eyes peering at me through the darkness.." "..the silence, frightening, teasing, chuckling at me for being so inadequate."

And another boy who wrote: ".. I tread through soft and crisp grass spurting with dew.." ".. (the fog) hits you like a burst balloon..". Or the boy from a broken home who, after a discussion on What Makes Me Happy. wrote: "To be out in the country cycling on a sunny day and the breeze behind me and the smell of fresh cut grass wilfing(!) around. And the sweet smell of flowers, mingling with that smell of the grass makes me happy without a doubt."

I must quote a few more, and remember, these are the no-hopers to whom school is just one more unpleasant authority which has, at best, to be tolerated, at worst, defied. "The shadows so straight, they seem to have been drawn with a ruler." "The morning. The early morning wakes up the school as it sits, plump on the ground, motionless." "The trees decorate the field with their long shadows." " A wide horizon, bumpy with the houses and their chimneys, which look as though they are just one millimetre apart between your fingers.!" "Seagulls fly back to sea, taking their shadows with them." And a girl wrote: "Seagulls, hunting for food, make very small shadows as they walk about the football pitch."

Most of this writing was in response to exercises I gave them: to look out of the classroom window and describe what they saw, or to describe what they might actually see or actually feel on a rainy or foggy day. The point of all this was to combat the stifling mediocrity of the pop culture they were and are subjected to, which destroys creativity and imagination and therefore dehumanises them. And all the teacher has to offer, against the billions spent on the above, is an appeal to their humanity based on a belief that it's there and that, despite their lowly status, they've got it too.

Another key activity with this group was the outside visit. I took them to the waterworks, the cement factory, Marley Tiles, Dentsply the false-teeth manufacturers in Lewes Rd., Marks and Spencer's and Forfar's the bakery. The idea was not to help these places recruit them, although some of them might perhaps have wanted to work there, but to show them what was going on in the area, how products and services on which they relied for their daily comfort and sustenance were produced and a general insight into the world of work. They were expected to write up their visit on our return. As it was a small class, I was usually able to take them all in the school mini-bus. Most of these places provided us with a slap-up tea at the end of the visit.

Towards the end of the school year, knowing how hard it was going to be for most of them to get a worthwhile job, I scouted round and made a few enquiries and set up some interviews, having first given some of them what I called interview drill. I also told them that if a reference was asked for they should tell the prospective employer to contact me. In this way, I felt that I was giving them as good a start as they might hope for and I did, indeed, receive several requests for references from a number of employers. I always stressed their strengths and hinted, as tactfully as possible, at their weaknesses, so that nobody could accuse me of pretending that they were angels. I know from feedback that it worked well in many cases.

Later someone else took over this Newsome work and I was given "normal" classes, usually First or Second Years. Each year was divided into streams. Yes, there were degrees even among these Eleven-plus "failures", that had to be sorted into sheep and goats. Some had "failed" less than others! Needless to say, those colleagues who were assigned the A Stream, either as class tutor or in their subject, had it somewhat easier, on the whole. I was usually put in charge of a B stream. Whether this was because I was deemed not good enough for the "cream" or too good, or unable to manage the Cs, I don't know and never asked.

It was whilst I had a group of one of these second-class failures that I came across a pupil with whom I am still in touch today. You will see him mentioned in the acknowledgements at the beginning of the book. It was during a class debate on: violence. He stood up and made a brief statement which still rings in my ears. His name was Michael and he was just over 12 years old. I got him to write up his speech, showed it to the Head and sent a copy to the Chief Education Officer. Here are a few excerpts:

"If God made this world he most definitely made violence."
"No human being can live without violence, any more than they can live without love."
"Wars (etc) are appalling, but...this is violence in its extreme."
"Religious people (should notice) that he (Jesus) once whipped people violently."
"Inside our body, violence and love fight a never-ending battle."

Just think of the maturity of that last quote. Michael also started writing poetry and, long after he had left my class, he used to hand me pieces he had written when we passed each other in the playground. These quotes are from a long poem about the horrors of war:

The Circle of Sorrow

" A thousand widows shed five hundred thousand tears"

"So many children left without a father,
Some are months and some are years.
The young are blind, they do not see their mother's tears."

"The road ahead will be so hard and long.
Daddy's gone. Daddy's gone."

But don't imagine for one moment that Michael was a limp-wristed aesthete, far from it. He was a large, muscular boy, quite outstanding at sport, captain of the school and Brighton Schools rugby teams, played basketball and was a competent boxer. After leaving school he became a member of Steve Ovett's athletics club and, now in his forties, he still runs regularly. There were many other "failures" who showed great ability and I shall not dwell any longer on this one outstanding pupil, except to say that, for a number of reasons, he left school with no paper qualifications whatsoever.

Later, at Evening classes, he obtained 'O' Level and 'A' Level certificates, went on to gain a degree at the Brighton Poly, as it then was, went further and studied for a post graduate teaching qualification and later, whilst pursuing a successful teaching career, did a post-graduate course for his MA. An exception? One who "slipped through the net"? Don't believe it. Michael is a one-man exposé of the whole eleven-plus swindle that denied, and in some areas still denies millions of children a proper, systematic education. And there are forces, even within the government, that want to re-introduce it where it has long since been consigned to the rubbish-heap!

Owing to a number of changes initiated by the Council *instead of* Comprehensive reform, amalgamation of some smaller schools with larger ones and a slight change in the structure of the system relating to the age of transfer from one stage to another, we had a number of new colleagues added to the staff. One was in my department, Bill Homer, ex-Indian Army and diligent explorer of historical minutiae. I got on very well with Bill, despite our quite different approach. He was a wonderful storyteller and was popular with the pupils although he insulted them right and left, albeit with a twinkle. His popularity was, alas, partly because he demanded little of them.

Another two new colleagues were Mary and Bill Chiappe, natives of Gibraltar. Bill was a potter and his pupils produced some really attractive pieces. Mary taught English and produced plays. I had a hand in one of these. It was Brecht's *Caucasian Chalk Circle* and I was given the job of rehearsing the chorus. I enjoyed this immensely and I honestly believe the actors did, too. Clarity of speech is one of my hobby-horses, so I was able to give free reign to my feelings. I stood or sat at the back of the hall and insisted that I should be able to hear every word, every syllable, clearly enunciated. It worked. When the famous, Brighton-based actress, Flora Robson, visited the performance, she particularly praised the choral speaking.

"That was Mr. Goldman's work ", piped up Ruby Besch, who happened to be within earshot. I also had the audacity to "improve" some of the translation, because I was dissatisfied with the idiom used.

The Chiappes became good friends, a friendship only marred by the fact that Mary usually beat me at table-tennis! They are both now teaching in Spain but I have one permanent reminder of Bill and his wit. He "threw" a lovely tankard for me as part of a presentation he arranged for the staff at the end of term. I was the rottenest darts player on the staff, or anywhere else for that matter, and he had inscribed on the pot: "Len Goldman - the most promising young player of the year". I was over 60 at the time.

The drama evenings were part of the school's social calendar, when parents were invited to witness some of the results of our efforts and, it was hoped, even enjoy themselves in the process. Other evenings were devoted to musical performances - the school had and has an excellent orchestra and two choirs. There was also the school Speech (or Prize-giving) Day. This was when proud parents turned up to see their offspring rewarded for successful effort.

The tradition remains. There is always an outside speaker, the choice of whom reflects the Head's leanings, and he himself gives his annual report. The Head Boy expresses the pupils' thanks to the staff and the Head Girl sings a hymn of praise for the outside speaker. This is followed by a buffet in the small hall. I have been retired for twenty years but I still attend these functions. Stringer is a school to which I have become emotionally attached.

It was, however, a Secondary Modern School. And loud though its advocates may claim that these schools were not "inferior" but just "different", everybody, including the pupils, knew that they existed to take the failures, the rejected. And this had its effect on the whole ethos of the school and, naturally, on the behaviour and willingness to learn of the pupils. And this notwithstanding the success of teachers in partly overcoming this handicap and, indeed, producing quite respectable GCE results from these "failures. So it behoved those of us who understood the nature of this artificially produced handicap to do something about it.

THE CAMPAIGN FOR COMPREHENSIVE SCHOOLS

The reader will have gathered that I am totally opposed to the whole Eleven-plus, Intelligence Testing, sorting and grading, chicanery that went on - and in some places still goes on - in our educational system. In short, I am opposed to selective education. It is not educational but political and, to use a favourite word of its supporters, ideological. They tried their best, by constantly "refining" and "improving" their methods but it didn't work because, by the very nature of human beings, it can't work. It attempted to forecast the whole future development of the child, acting like God, and you can't do that even with the middle-aged, let alone children.

The proof of this was plain for those with eyes to see, every day of the week in our schools and universities. After a while, teachers in the schools where the pupils were supposed to be "unable to profit from a Grammar School education" began to ignore this mantra and to teach at least some children, those not too damaged by their rejection via the Eleven-plus, to the 'O' level syllabus with a view to entering them for this "Grammar School examination". And some of the results were highly instructive and, at the very least, contradicted the confident forecasts of testers.

I shall not dwell on these facts but quoting them is important for what follows. As I remarked above, I was appalled when I came to Brighton and found a widespread attitude of hostility to the whole idea of Comprehensives. So I was delighted when I discovered that a Brighton Campaign for Comprehensive Schools had just been newly formed. I joined it immediately and became one of an initially small band of enthusiasts. We met in the front room of Professor Jimmy Sang's house in Surrenden Crescent. Jimmy was a Scot teaching and researching genetics in the biology department at Sussex University. The significance of having an internationally known geneticist on our side in the debate about "intelligence", will not be lost on the reader. Sadly, Jimmy has just recently died and merited a lengthy and laudatory obit in the Guardian. Oddly however, it did not mention his participation in the above campaign.

One of his colleagues, Dr. Les Allen, a physics lecturer and laser expert who later won acclaim for his work in that field, was also a keen participator in the campaign.. These academics were obviously bright boys who had been winners in our divided and competitive schools' system and yet, from their own experience, they were opposed to it. Several local councillors were also in the Campaign. There was Stanley Deason, an alderman and elder statesman, respected even by his political opponents; Francis Tonks, later to be a Labour parliamentary candidate and, later still, mayor of Brighton, was also one of our promoters and activists, as was Jennifer Platt (later Goldie), lecturer at the university's School of Social Sciences. Councillor Ray Blackwood, though not officially one of our members, took an active interest from the start and frequently discussed points with me before making his contribution to the debates on the subject in the council chamber - on one memorable occasion, getting me out of bed to talk it over on the 'phone!

Francis Tonks and Les Allen,
Comprehensive school camaigners

    Although the government had issued an Order, that all LEAs should prepare plans for school reorganisation "on Comprehensive lines", the instruction was sufficiently vague and allowed considerable leeway, so that Tory councils like ours and no doubt some Labour ones as well could delay its implementation or, as ours did after some time, introduce changes that fell far short of Comprehensivisation, simply tinkered with ages of transfer from one stage to the next or even suggested "Comprehensive Schools" side by side with Grammar Schools!. With a blare of trumpets, they announced that there would now be First Schools, from 5 to 8; Middle Schools, from 8 to

12; and High Schools, from 12 to 16, which was, by then, the compulsory minimum school leaving age.

The Campaign issued informative material, ran public meetings and did its best to stir up controversy in the staff rooms, within the council and, especially, the Education Committee and Schools' Sub-committee and among the general public. Our meetings were publicised and reported on in The Argus and elsewhere, with pictures of the speakers and quotes from their arguments. Detailed reports were also given of council meetings and decisions and the issue was kept well and truly in the public domain. The Argus was, on the whole, supportive and, in July 1970, when a Tory government was again in charge, it printed a leader which castigated the council and the minister (Margaret Thatcher!) thus: Brighton LEA was "among the most backward and reactionary in Britain" and Mrs. Thatcher gave them "carte blanche to ... do nothing."

Letters galore were written to the paper and the overwhelming majority supported our campaign. There were, however, some quite vituperative "anti" letters. I must quote from one classic example. The writer asserted that we Campaigners were in it either for political or financial(!) gain, that we had an inferiority complex, that we hoped our geese would become swans, that we were doctrinaire ignoramuses who thought any change must be good and, finally, that we hadn't realised that there must be selection, even in Comprehensive Schools. I ought to have had that letter framed.

Ex-Grammar School pupils were among our most determined opponents. Why spoil good schools? they asked. On one memorable occasion, during a Labour Party Conference, we organised a large meeting with Edward Redhead, Minister of State at the DES, as the main speaker. I wasn't too happy with his less than forthright exposition of the case we had been putting much more succinctly I felt, but it certainly gave a boost to our campaign, despite the fact that a boorish Tory lout tried to disrupt proceedings by chatting, in a loud voice, to his companion throughout the meeting.

We also offered to address meetings of trade unions or LP or Co-op branches and, on one unique occasion, a Conservative Party branch. I found quite a few sceptics in the Labour Party at that time, indeed many of the leadership were still sold on the idea that the Grammar Schools provided a "way out" for the "gifted" working-class child. When I addressed the LP branch of which an old Labour stalwart who shall be nameless was a member, his only remark after my speech was to the effect that "people aren't interested in education" and "there's no votes in it"! And yet, a Gallup poll as early as December 1966 showed that half the population were in favour of Comprehensives and only 22% against!

Our main opponent and, we felt, the real stumbling block to progress on the issue, was Dr. Stone, the Chief Education Officer. He was an official of the old school. I saw him as an elitist in the extreme. Why try to promote dullards when only intellects like him and the chosen few were able to excel academically? Of course, he never expressed it in those stark terms. They seldom do. It's all wrapped up in the pseudo-scientific jargon beloved of those who believe in selective education. And, although Dr. Stone was later superseded by Kenneth Antcliffe, a younger, more open-minded colleague, there was still a long way to go.

The local NUT Association (the BTA) was also involved and they devoted considerable time and energy to debating what kind of scheme would be best suited to Brighton and what would be the most effective way of bringing it about. They were later joined by the local National Association of Schoolmasters (usually a deadly rival) and Barry Gooders, its secretary, played a big part in what the Argus called the "battle". The national Comprehensive Schools Committee, under their secretary, Caroline Benn (Tony's wife) kept in touch and gave support and encouragement.

One method the Campaign adopted was to divide the councillors into small groups and assign a member to each group. The idea was to tackle each of your little group individually on the whole subject. Of the two councillors who fell to my lot, one was a former Labour man who had gone over to the Tories and the other a property developer. The first one turned up at my house one Saturday morning with his son, also a councillor. I sat them in my armchairs and harangued them for some considerable time. I pointed out the iniquities of the divided system and the advantages of the change we were proposing. They showed little serious interest, made a few fairly irrelevant comments and the young man remarked that he'd gone to a Secondary Modern School and it hadn't done him any harm.

I went to see the second councillor in his office. He made a great show of sorting papers and files and generally "being busy" and, after my little speech, he remarked, rather drily, that he wasn't so interested in education as his area of responsibility lay elsewhere. He added, as an aside, that he sent his sons to Public School, though this may have been said apologetically, as if to say: "I know I'm biased." Fair enough, but I reminded him that, as a councillor, he was also a member of the Education Authority and thus responsible for everything that went on in the town's schools, so therefore if he wasn't interested in education he ought not to be a councillor.

George Humphreys, a leading Labour councillor, produced a pamphlet explaining the meaning of and the need for the desired change entitled: *Comprehensives in Brighton? Why and How*, and the Trades Council also organised meetings in support and there were demonstrations in Churchill Square and elsewhere. An Open Forum was held which set up a Comprehensive Schools Action Council, that went on to organise a large demonstration at a council meeting. It was supported by the Trades Council, the NUT, the Schoolmasters' organisation as well as the one for teachers in technical colleges and, of course, not forgetting our own Campaign. Brian Jones, a lecturer at the Tech', was its secretary. A petition was hastily organised by the Campaign and although only taken round one small area because of shortage of time, it was signed by 3,000 people. We have a picture of Bernard Besch (who, with his wife Ruby, had been a tremendous campaigner for the cause) handing in a massive bulk of paper to the then mayor. The latter worthy could hardly help being impressed.

Children parading 1966

The council simply could no longer ignore the wishes of large numbers of its constituents. It fell back on the time-honoured technique of producing something like a new scheme, but which still retained the hated selective

118

process. One scheme followed another, but in the end the Comprehensive protagonists, who now included all the main teacher organisations except the "Joint Four" (i.e. the "Grammar School" unions) as well as parents and students, compelled the council to come up with an acceptable plan for real Comprehensives - the present system, in fact.

So the Campaign, which had lasted nearly ten years, was finally successful. The council still had a Tory majority but many of them had now become convinced of the need for a change. Indeed, when it came to the decisive debate, one Tory councillor, Professor Kingman, made the best speech of the evening in favour of the Comprehensive scheme. The result was that, starting officially in 1974 (but phased-in in 1973) all Secondary Moderns were to become Comprehensives, as was the girls' Varndean Grammar School, which became mixed. The boys' Varndean was transformed into a Sixth Form College, as was Brighton Hove and Sussex Grammar School, in Dyke Rd. and affectionately known thereafter as BHASVIC. Westlain (Grammar) joined with Stanmer to become Falmer Comprehensive, which retained its Sixth Form for about 15 years until it was no longer viable and from then on its pupils wishing to continue went to one of the Colleges,.

I was not entirely satisfied. I would have preferred all-through Comprehensives as we had in London, so that the top two forms of seventeen- and eighteen-year-olds could act as an example to the rest of the school with many of them going off to university when they left. They could also help in giving leadership to the younger pupils and - perhaps most important of all - encourage the school to recruit teachers of the highest academic calibre.

But this was a relatively minor cavil as against the great advance represented by the change. A more important question related to the inner organisation of each school. There were two main aspects to be resolved. Firstly, how the school was to be departmentalised, and this had an effect on the salaries of those involved. Secondly, how the pupils were to be divided up. And each school was independent in these matters or, to put it more bluntly, each Head made his or her own decisions, irrespective of what other Heads were doing. Comprehensive education in Brighton was a maze of contradictions. It had been introduced by a Tory council, whose party nationally, though paying lip-service to the idea, was really dead against it. The impetus in Brighton was three-fold. Our Campaign had roused public consciousness on the issue and any council must be mindful of public feeling. There was a national move in that direction, one LEA after another introducing the scheme in one form or another.

But, perhaps most decisive, the schools were about to be taken over by East Sussex who might well have a scheme up their sleeve which would not be to the liking of their Brighton counterpart. So, after an interesting debate, the split scheme, High Schools (12 and, later, 11 to 16) and Sixth Form Colleges (16 to 18), proposed by the Education Committee, was accepted by the council, which rightly concluded that the new LEA would not want to disrupt a scheme that was already running.

Another contradiction was that, although the new organisation had been brought in for the above reasons, they were not necessarily going to trust the new type of school to those who had advocated them. Did the Heads of these schools, some of them newly appointed, really believe in the Comprehensive principle? I know of two (who shall be nameless) who had opposed these schools right up to the last minute and yet were only too happy to accept a leadership role in them! I had been a leading advocate of Comprehensive reform for ten years and yet I didn't even get on to one of the sub-committees formed to determine their character and inner organisation.

The result was that, with some exceptions, the schools were run almost like three different schools under one roof and with one Head. To add to this, at the end of each year, there was what I called the upses and downses. Although the streaming was based on tests rather similar to the Intelligence Test, it was found that, after a year's instruction, some pupils were "misplaced" and had to be moved up or down to rectify this. The strange thing was and is that there were just the right number of "A" children, "B" children etc to fill the available places in those classes, just as in the divided school system that the Comprehensives were supposed to replace.

In this connection, it is worth quoting from a survey issued in January 1970 by the National Foundation for Educational Research, after five years of study. They found that, in Primary Schools, streaming made no difference to academic success but adversely affected the attitudes and the emotional and social development of those in the lower streams. In unstreamed schools their confidence and attitude to the teachers improved greatly, especially where the teachers really believed in the method. The study also revealed that some 15% were "in the wrong stream", anyway, and that those placed in higher streams tended to improve whilst those in the lower streams deteriorated. As I frequently maintained in argument with my colleagues: tell a child it's a dunce, with the full weight of the educational establishment behind you, and it will believe you - and behave accordingly. The findings of the NFER survey merely confirmed what I knew in my bones already.

Further evidence of the debilitating effect of streaming was provided at a lecture I attended addressed by Prof. Hilde Himmelweit, an educational psychologist. She had made a study of 500 pupils from London Grammar Schools, the starting point of which was that the streaming process differed in each school and that, consequently, those in one stream in one school might have been in quite a different stream had they been in a different school. But, and this was the point, the stream they were in had a profound effect not just on their attitude and performance but especially on their *aspirations*. She followed the careers of these youngsters right through until they were twenty-five, so was able to see exactly what they had made of their lives up to that point. The inescapable conclusion was that if they had been in a different school and therefore possibly in a different stream, their careers might have been quite different. Perhaps this was unimportant for those from top streams - but what about the others?

So there was streaming in Brighton's brand new Comprehensives. Plus ça change? Not quite. Despite this clinging on to old ideas, too deeply entrenched to be jettisoned, the new schools were vastly superior to the old ones. In spite of everything, the pupils did mix, especially in sport and other cultural activities and I found that aspirations could be fostered far better than in the Secondary Modern School. Of course, there were now pupils from a much wider range of social and intellectual backgrounds and a number of them were very advanced indeed. There were also a greater number able to express ideas of their own, on education and everything else.

STRINGER - SECONDARY MODERN TO COMPREHENSIVE

And here, perhaps, I should turn from the general to the particular, i.e. to my own school, Dorothy Stringer. Ted Hood had already retired and a new Deputy had been appointed. He was a small, thin, very pale-faced man with a wide forehead that seemed to dominate his somewhat peaky features. His grey-blue eyes glowed intently and he was rather keen on the cane. That his judgement was sometimes flawed is evidenced by a remark he made about a boy in my History Fifth year. I had wondered aloud why this boy had not been chosen as a prefect (a newly-introduced practice). "Oh. he's just a yobbo", he replied. That "yobbo" went on to gain a degree and then an MSc in Engineering and is now an experienced civil engineer! Just by the way, of course, he was also an Eleven-plus "failure".

I think the introduction of Comprehensive Schools, with all the re-organisation that would mean, was too much for Mr. Carter. Anyway, he resigned and a new Head took over a year before the big change took place, i.e. in 1973. The change-over was accompanied by the biggest "general post" in the history of Brighton's teachers. All teachers lost their previous positions and had to re-apply for them. The effect of this was that one could apply for any of the new posts that were being created as well as the old ones which were retained in the system.

So, although we all "lost" our jobs, we could apply for the many better ones that were now on offer! Apply, yes, but it became clear that there were a number of "blue-eyed boys" who had already been chosen for the plum jobs. Having applied for and failed to get (despite being told that I "interviewed well") several higher posts, I was eventually graciously granted - my own job back!

Mr. Carter's successor was Michael Hodell; *Mr*. Hodell, to you. He was a Tory councillor in Mid-Sussex. He outlined his plans to the staff at an introductory meeting organised for him by Mr.Carter. It seemed he was a bit of a whizz kid when it came to school management. He was well up on the latest managerial techniques and I came to realise that his organisational skills were formidable. He had obviously read up on the subject extensively. He was also determined to get his own way; as he so elegantly put it: "Those who can't stand the heat should get out of the kitchen!"

Of medium height and considerable bulk, he had a large impressive head, with his abundant, fair hair going back in neat waves, and affected a largish beard. One wag on the staff, some time later, christened him "Big Daddy" but I don't think the nickname stuck. He presented himself very well, always clad in an academic gown and, indeed, had an aura of the stage about him. I think parents and the public in general were impressed: he looked every inch the Headmaster. I must also record, because it gives a deeper insight into the man's thinking, that, on one occasion at morning assembly he recounted a story that gave a social message quite contrary to what I understand as the Tory outlook, encapsulated in Mrs.Thatcher's famous remark: "There is no such thing as society".

The story is supposedly a Chinese one. A man died and went to hell. There was a table with wonderful delicacies and soups of various kinds. But you only had knives, forks and spoons a yard long, making it impossible to help yourself. All starved. Transferred to heaven (by some means I have forgotten), he was faced with the same situation. There, however, each person used the awkward cutlery to help his neighbour to eat and drink. A lesson in social co-operation that could have been preached by any communist! There was clearly more to Mr. H than met the eye.

He divided the school into large departments, rather like university faculties, in which several of the former departments were grouped. In my case, History, Geography and Religious Education were placed in the Humanities Department which was headed by George Montgomery, another longstanding friend of mine. The hospitality and kindness shown to us by him and his artistic and highly talented wife, Judith, really deserves a chapter on its own. The salary implications of George's new appointment were clear. The Head of this new department received the appropriate salary, whilst the former departmental Heads were demoted to being "in charge" of their subject and were rewarded accordingly. It was all worked out on a points system and, because the new Head wanted to use some points for new posts he had created, there weren't enough left to pay these lowered echelons properly.

Later, there was a change in policy. A new post of Director of Studies was created for George, whose organisational flair and IT skills at last received recognition and he carried out his new extensive duties brilliantly. George had been Head of PE when I first arrived but later, after gaining a high qualification in Geography, had taken over that department. What impressed me was his attention to detail and his insistence on the highest standards from the pupils. He had a careful and logical approach which paid dividends. The Head was also obviously impressed and that was why he'd made George Head of Humanities. After taking over his new post, he combined the two responsibilities for a time but this was soon seen to be untenable, the Humanities department was abandoned and I was again made subject Head with a consequent rise in salary.

One innovation which the new Head introduced was European Studies for the whole Fifth Year. All the teachers in Humanities contributed a syllabus for this new discipline. The Head was an enthusiastic member of the European Movement and, of course, a supporter of the Common Market that his party had espoused. (Interesting, considering the Tories' present stance on Europe!) It was because I suspected that this was the real motive for this new subject that I entertained grave doubts about the necessity for it.

Nonetheless, I took great pains to prepare a syllabus of outstanding events in European History, as well as making a list of every European country and its capital, finding out a few things I didn't know, myself, in the process. Once a week, apart from the individual lessons in our own subjects, we had the whole Year group in the hall to listen to a lecture from one of us. Very often, we showed films or used some other visual materials to give colour and extra interest to the talk. My own two contributions were lectures on The Rise of Fascism and on Lenin and the Russian Revolution. Looking back, I realise that, despite my early misgivings, I actually enjoyed the challenge this new subject presented.

When the Deputy left to take up a headship elsewhere, a new Deputy Head, Peter Shephard, took over. He was from Derbyshire, very solidly built, played tennis and, I believe, had been a rugby player in his youth. He was plain-speaking, jovial and likeable. He became the Head's right-hand man, a faithful lieutenant. The policy of this - and most other - Brighton Comprehensives - was one of determined streaming, slightly softened by having parallel streams within each year, i.e. three streams of three classes each, making nine classes in each year. This was possible because the total number of pupils topped the thousand.

Now, whilst I disclaim any attempt to propagandise the pupils or use my position to influence them in any but a humane way (as preached at assemblies - but not always practised by those who did the preaching!) it wasn't long before the more perceptive of my charges "found me out" so to speak. I have a feeling that some of them saw me as, at best, a well-meaning progressive and, at worst, something of a fuddy-duddy old "Leftie", believing in persuasion and mass - but peaceful - action, whilst their mentors, often Trotskyites, seemed to promise dramatic action more attractive to the young. Nonetheless, I made friends with a number of them, some visiting me at home for a chat. I also got to know a number of parents, some of whom were Labour Party activists. On one occasion, when I was on a CND demonstration in London, I wasn't particularly surprised to see a number of my pupils also taking part - and I don't think they were surprised to see me there, either.

Some of them still stand out in my memory. There was Lawrence, a lanky, sporting type, a fast bowler to boot, who was quite outstanding intellectually, too. He was the only one who ever got *more than full marks* in a trial examination! The point was that extra marks could be awarded for exceptionally good answers, in order to make up for lower marks in some other question. But Lawrence didn't get low marks for any of the other questions, hence the apparently impossible score. Then there was the German girl who'd come to England at an early age, was completely bi-lingual and also excelled in my subject. She knew the answers almost before I asked the question. Coming from a country - and no doubt a family - where the intellect is highly prized, must be an important factor in her high achievement. A number of the pupils were children of local councillors, Jonathan, for example. His work was exemplary, often more detailed than one could reasonably expect, at his age - and he was politically very active.

So was Ezri, a Jewish boy, son of a rabbi. His imagined account as a Norman combatant at the Battle of Hastings began: " My horse sniffed the evening air and blew through his nostrils.." He later recruited me to the Anti-nazi League! Then there was Stephen who, I seem to remember, when in his First Year, went up to London, to visit the British Museum, in order to give a really full answer to a question, on, I think, Ancient Egypt. In his answer, he quoted from the inscription in the glass case whose contents he had clearly studied minutely. Naturally, like the others I have mentioned, when he got to the Fifth Year, he - and they - did brilliantly in their 'O' Levels and went on, two years later, to university and obtained first class degrees.

Stephen won a scholarship to Oxford, where he helped to set up a debating society in competition with the traditional, rather exclusive one. Lawrence got an Exhibition at Cambridge. Another boy I should mention, though not one of the outstanding intellectuals, was obviously enjoying his school experience. His name was Glenn. He was in my History group and his devotion to the tasks set was exemplified by the project he carried out on Leonardo da Vinci, with appropriate illustrations and even some research. He certainly wasn't overawed by the spectacularly brainy. Today, some twenty years later, Glenn is a highly successful estate agent.

I must also mention Holly, who first came to my notice when she took the lead in the school production of Brecht's *Caucasian Chalk Circle*, mentioned above. As a budding actress, Holly gave off a certain hint of glamour and it may have been her preoccupation with histrionics that tended to make her a little inattentive in class which I occasionally found irritating but she was highly intelligent (in the best sense) and we generally got on very well, especially as she knew of my interest in the theatre which, I'm afraid, meant that I sometimes made her late for her next lesson when we got deep into the subject of our mutual interest. Holly was also in my History group and did creditably in the exam She never did make it on the stage and, at present, she's in Australia, successfully producing marketable artistic items.

Supervising a rehearsal of
The Caucasian Chalk Circle 1977

Cast of *A Midsummer Night's Dream* at Stringer 1980

In the Fifth Year, in my History class, I dared to mix pupils from all the streams. This was particularly risky and difficult because they had been so thoroughly streamed (mentally as well as physically) all the way through the school, that the lower ones could easily feel out of their depth and the bright ones could get bored with my efforts to stimulate their "inferiors". So I had to tread a fine line between these two dangers. Sometimes it worked, sometimes it didn't. But one thing is clear, the accusation against my method: that it would hold back the clever ones, was proved false by the very results I quoted above. And I am quite certain that some of the poorer pupils did better than they would have done in a low stream, where expectations are low.

A number of new colleagues joined the staff, many of them from Moulsecoomb School, both prior to and just after the re-organisation. My first thoughts turn to Mick Hickman, son of a colleague whom I knew as treasurer of the local NUT association. Mick was just out of university and joined me in the History Department. Though a novice, his teaching ability was considerable. His historical knowledge was admirable and his power of factual recall phenomenal. He was also an excellent tennis player. We worked on a revision of the History syllabus together and became, and have remained, firm friends.

His other subject was Religious Education - he was a lay preacher in the local Methodist church and was to become Senior Circuit Steward - and later he was promoted to Head of RE (now RS), a position he retains to this day. He declared himself politically a Liberal and, as I later discovered, a supporter of monarchy, perhaps as a barrier to revolution. So we had much to disagree and argue about, though never acrimoniously. Indeed, he had me along to his Methodist youth group a couple of times. On one occasion I spoke on: The Spirit of Marxism, in which I tried to show that Christians are not the only ones who believe in the spirit - the *human* spirit - and that "man does not live by bread alone". It is hardly a postscript to add that Mick has become a very effective teacher.

Another newcomer, who had been Deputy Head at Moulsecoomb, was Jim Catchpole, a Geordie with a mining background. Jim, who taught Geography, was tall and athletic looking and was full of energy and organisational skills. Apart from his official teaching duties, he was a great one for trips abroad and many pupils benefited from this. On one memorable occasion Rita and I and Fleur (yes, we'd produced a daughter by this time) took part in one of these journeys. It was to Carinthia in Austria, in a hotel near a wonderful lake. I remember it particularly as our knowledge of German enabled us to smooth out certain difficulties which arose, and because of the great pleasure of swimming in the lake.

Some of my work had been in the English Department, one of the three former departments which, because of their size, still retained their old status. Its Head was Jo Bolton, a native of Yorkshire, who'd graduated at Oxford. She was short and dark, with very bright eyes, had a slightly refined northern accent and always looked neat and competent. Her views seemed to me very much those of the Establishment and we disagreed profoundly on educational questions but we always had a pleasant word for each other. Some years later, we were all devastated when Jo died of cancer.

A newcomer to the English Department deserves a special mention because she turned out to be one of the most effective and talented teachers I have come across in the whole of my career. Julia McGirr had such sensitivity to and an empathy with the pupils that they responded with affection and, more importantly, a willingness to learn. And the ability of a teacher to evoke that response is a hallmark of professional competence. It took some

128

time for her abilities to be recognised but, eventually, she was made Head of the department and remained in that position until, under a new headmaster, she was made responsible for the further development of teaching skills in the school. She held this post until her recent retirement.

One of the out-of-school activities Julia pursued was a debating and discussion group, with which I enthusiastically co-operated. Teams were entered for the competition run by the English-speaking Society and the outstanding success of some of these teams was a tribute not only to the commitment of the pupils concerned but also to her initiative. I helped in whatever ways I could and was delighted that our "Comprehensive kids" beat the experienced and confident students of some of the posh local Public Schools. Of the many first-class contributions of our teams, I would single out two prominent ones, the two Jonathans. One brilliantly proposed a motion condemning the use of animals in the development of commercial products such as, for example, shampoo, whilst the other one gave a witty talk and a devastating critique of television. There had recently been a blackout of TV, due, I think, to a strike, and he opened his remarks by an amusing reference to this pause in our viewing and developed his argument from there: a perfect example of seizing the moment by citing an appropriately current event.

As a committed union activist, I attended my first meeting of the Brighton Teachers' Association, where Ted Hood was the secretary and Mr. Carter was our co-opted representative on the Education Committee. The president and secretary were always invited to a mayoral strawberries-and-cream party on the Pavilion lawns in the summer and, in turn, were part of a group which invited the mayor and certain councillors to a dinner and dance in the Pavilion itself. The local association even met in the Education Offices, courtesy of the council. A nice, cosy arrangement! Who'd want to upset the applecart by making militant noises about pay and conditions, size of classes and - God forbid - Comprehensive Schools? Who would? I would, of course and I feel confident that by doing so I played some small part, at least, in the happy outcome of the Comprehensive Schools Campaign, described above. I soon discovered that there were one or two others, especially Erica Stratta and the Besches, who felt the same way that I did.

At my very first meeting, I even had the temerity to oppose allowing a suggestion to go through on the nod, that we prioritise a motion for conference that our own association had put forward - before I came along, that is. The president that year was "Becky" Beckworth, gorgeously attired in a large hat, as was the wont in those days. And I could see that she took my intervention rather badly. These days, when we are both retired and good friends, she sometimes twits me about it. What was worse, the meeting agreed with me and the motion, our "own" motion, was not prioritised.

Ted Hood had a few words with me back at school in private, making a joke of it but I could see that he was not too pleased. After that, the meetings were the scene of real, hard discussions not, perhaps, quite so genteel as heretofore, but friendly, nonetheless. It soon became clear that the times were changing and real struggles both with the government and the local council were on the order of the day. The BTA committee, whose membership previously was the prerogative of a cosy little clique, was soon joined by Erica and somewhat later by me. I can't remember all the details but the BTA's policy gradually took on a more determined aspect when it came to national issues, especially salaries. When Ted Hood retired and, rather reluctantly, gave up the secretaryship, Bill Harris, Head of Patcham Junior School, took over and things were livened up considerably.

It was shortly after this that I was elected President of the Association. In my presidential address, I took the opportunity to do two things. Firstly, to lampoon what I called "the grim brothers of the council chamber" for their attempts at that time to introduce cocked-up schemes of re-organisation that fell far short of real Comprehensives. And, secondly, to outline my vision of the best possible education for all, basing myself on what was happening in the school system in the GDR - though I didn't mention it by name — where the parents and the whole community were involved with "their" school and every child was expected to sit a school-leaving exam which laid the basis for further training in whichever direction they wanted to go, to satisfy social needs as well as their own. I should also mention that, having resumed my teaching career in England, I again started selling the Party's educational journal, Education Today and Tomorrow, to my colleagues at school and in the union.

Before leaving the subject of my involvement in education, a word about the examination system at the time is, perhaps, appropriate. On my return to Britain, there was still only one official national examination taken in schools, the GCE, at Ordinary Level for the 16-year-olds and, for those who stayed on voluntarily to 18, at Advanced Level. Soon after my return, however, a new exam was created, for those considered unable to attain the GCE. This was called the Certificate of Secondary Education (CSE). Since one of its History syllabuses covered the same period of Economic History as its GCE counterpart, I was able to teach my "mixed" Fourth and Fifth Years and delay the decision as to which exam each pupil was to sit until the very last moment.

In some cases I entered a pupil for both exams. This had one unintended consequence: I was able to compare the pupil's results in the two exams. Now, a Grade 1 at CSE was supposed to be the equivalent of a pass in GCE. But it didn't always work that way. One pupil scored less than a 1 in CSE but passed his GCE. In one exceptional case, a boy who only got a 2 in CSE did very well in GCE. My point? Firstly, that exam results are only a very rough indication of a candidate's abilities and, secondly, the relationship between the two exams was not nearly so clear-cut as was claimed. Soon after its inception, I was delegated by my union to sit on the South-East Region Examination Board (SEREB) of the CSE and attended a monthly meeting at its HQ in Tunbridge Wells. A very instructive experience!

After I retired I continued to be a member of this Board and to take part in the discussions leading up to what many of us had always desired: one examination for all 16+ candidates. Here, all the old questions about intelligence, pupils' abilities to pass exams, how to sort out the various levels of achievement, and so on, came to the fore. Many doubted the possibility or the wisdom of having one examination for all. The strongest argument in favour was that the existence of Comprehensive Schools made it necessary.

The upshot was the General Certificate of Secondary Education (GCSE), with 7 grades instead of 5 and in which it would be assumed that the first three grades were equivalent to the old GCE at "O" Level and the bottom four, to CSE. There were to be questions at different levels, with grades to match, and candidates could opt for whichever level they felt confident of tackling. My view is that the greater the refinement of grading, the greater the danger of reverting to different levels of schooling, the very thing that Comprehensives were designed to avoid, especially in view of what I have recorded above when the two exams existed in parallel. Five grades would be ample and, even then, not too much significance should be attached to them. As this runs counter to prevailing established wisdom, there will be a long hard road before the rationality of it is accepted. However, despite the fact that I am now considered to be out of the fight, I shall obstinately continue to keep the matter in the public eye.

POLITICS AGAIN

The war had been a catalyst. What had changed since then? Almost full employment, for one thing, an unprecedented level of prosperity, for another. Workers were taking holidays abroad, even owning property abroad. The distribution of consumer goods was, consequently, far higher than anything which had been achieved before the war. Were workers still being "exploited"? Clearly, a lot of them didn't think so. Was revolution still on the cards? And would it be violent or peaceful? And if we modified our policies what effect would this have on our relationship with parties in other countries with whom we were linked and, in particular, with the Soviet Union and the other socialist countries?

This was a period when dramatic political changes were taking place, both nationally and internationally. The Khrushchev exposé of Stalin's megalomania had also been a catalyst that, firstly, led many of us to re-appraise our attitude to the USSR and then to take a hard look at all our policies on both foreign and home affairs. Marxists believe in the utmost flexibility because of the constantly changing nature of reality. We have our very firm principles but they have to be applied in a changing world. Nature experiences changes and so does human society. Had we become too rigid? Too wedded to certain practices and methods of analysis?

And then came Hungary. Dissatisfaction there with the ruling Party and its policies, seen as a result of Soviet domination, was taken advantage of by Right-wing (in some cases semi-fascist) elements but they were also supported by wide sections of the population, including many who regarded themselves as genuine Marxists. The resultant upheaval led to street demonstrations and violent clashes, especially with the security forces, and the Party lost control. This was a grave danger to the whole security set-up carefully organised by the Soviet Union after the war, so they sent in troops who restored the former government to power. Our Party supported this action as "antifascist", citing the dangers of a Third World War. The EC's stance was opposed by what became known as the New Thinkers in the Party but supported by the mainstream as well as the hardliners.

In short, there was tremendous controversy within the Party, fertile ground for splits and factionalism, just the thing we had always tried to avoid.

The Party had already produced a major new policy document called: The British Road to Socialism. It marked a distinct break with certain past formulations and had been strongly opposed by individuals and groups who saw it as a betrayal. Violent revolution was not envisaged and the peaceful transfer of power would be by parliamentary means but would encompass extra-parliamentary activity, such as that undertaken by CND, the trade-union movement, peace organisations and so on.

The socialist idea was still dominant and the critique of capitalism remained. The control of our livelihood as well as nearly all means of information and communication by private, profit-making institutions was still seen as the major obstacle to social advance and the takeover of "the outstanding heights of industry, commerce and finance" by "the people" was the ultimate aim. But there would be no Soviet style "dictatorship of the proletariat" which, in effect, had meant "by the Party" and there would be no barrier to opposition groups, who would have full freedom to operate, within the law, of course. A large-scale campaign to popularise the British Road was undertaken.

It should be remembered that the Cold War was in full swing. In America, the Un-American-Activities Committee was rooting out supposed communists (with or without a capital c) persecuting and branding them as enemies of "the American Way of Life" and hounding them out of public life. This was especially true in Hollywood, where many progressive actors and producers had produced some fine films exposing the rottenness in parts of American society. The *Grapes of Wrath* was one obvious example. This gave rise to the case of the so-called Hollywood Ten. Those who refused to name any colleague who they knew to be in the Party were actually jailed as were a number of others simply for being active in the trade-union or labour movement. Apparently, it's not difficult in the US to frame such people on quite spurious other charges, as none of these activities were illegal. After all, America is a "free country".

This atmosphere of suspicion and accusation was, to a somewhat lesser extent, mirrored in Britain. Our Civil Service was combed for "subversives" and many comrades were demoted or even sacked, especially if they were in sensitive jobs. It is not easy to prove victimisation but I'm pretty sure that my own advancement in the Brighton education system was,

134

at any rate, not helped by my activities in the NUT and, especially my espousal of the Comprehensive cause. This was hinted to me privately many times. But England is a much more liberal place than America and my job was never in danger.

In Brighton the Party branch secretary was Margery Chaplin, an elderly comrade of unfailing good humour but considerable firmness of purpose. The branch engaged in a variety of activities; we supported the miners' strike and organised meetings in the town for this purpose, with Gordon McClennan, the Party General Secretary, speaking at one which was packed out. We also helped to organise demonstrations against the Vietnam War. Due to lack of resources, it was often left to individuals to attach themselves to various causes and encourage the other comrades and, if possible, the whole branch, to support them. My activities on the education front were a case in point.

Another example would be that of Eileen Daffern, a colleague who taught French in Westlain Grammar School and later worked in the Schools' European Studies unit, based in the university. Eileen flung herself into the Brighton Peace Movement and rapidly became its king(or queen?)pin, later setting up and leading the Sussex Alliance for Nuclear Disarmament (SAND). Now in her late eighties, Eileen is still fighting the good fight. She is currently writing her memoirs but I do not know if she will follow my example and publish them.

Stanley Harrison was another stalwart of the Party who was in our branch. Stan was a journalist of immense experience and had written a book about the struggle for a free press through the ages entitled: *Poor Men's Guardians*. In it he quotes from G. J. Harney, the Chartist leader, who described what happened when power had passed from the old ruling class to the new prosperous middle class: "More crafty than the men of force, the men of fraud had recourse to corruption in lieu of persecution; and the Press, from being the pioneer of Progress and the champion of Right, became the lackey of oppression and the relentless enemy of Eternal Justice." Written 160 years ago, how aptly those sentiments apply today! I greatly admired Stan's diligent research and found him stimulating company. Sadly, he died a few years ago.

Some members were extremely sectarian. One of these was an elderly comrade called Morrie Bellos, an old friend from London days. I was very fond of old Morrie but I could not possibly approve of his bitter condemnation of anything which he considered deviated from "the line". And any criticism of the Soviet Union was taboo.

It was about this time that the first damaging split occurred in the Party. A group of comrades, mainly based in the Surrey District, broke away and formed the New Communist Party and published a paper called The New Worker. Their complaint seemed to be that, with the publication of *The British Road to Socialism*, and subsequent tendencies, the Party had betrayed its origins and its leaders were traitors to the class struggle.

Our secretary, Margery, joined them. Morrie, who might have been expected to do so, did not immediately follow her. The branch convened a meeting, addressed by Reuben Falber, by now a member of the Party's Executive Committee and, after a serious discussion, passed a resolution condemning the move and affirming our overall agreement with the policies being pursued. I remember contributing to the discussion with an outline of the changes in the situation that necessitated the new direction in which we were moving.

Now that Margery had defected to the NCP, another secretary had to be sought. It was quite an onerous responsibility and there was no clamour to be elected, it was much more a question of persuading someone to volunteer. In the end, Pearl Myers stepped into the breach. Pearl was a Londoner as was her husband, Peter, a travelling salesman. She was very forthright, given to unparliamentary language and full of confidence. They were a very sociable couple and great parties were enjoyed at their flat in St. George's St., Kemp Town. We put up candidates at local elections, not because there was much chance of overcoming the enormous advantages held by the larger, established parties, but because it was an opportunity to present our policies to the local population and, in any case, participation in elections was the mark of a serious political party. I did a certain amount of the necessary legwork at these times but, in general, my election activity was - and is - largely devoted to assisting Labour Party candidates.

Some years later, another split occurred. It centred round control of the Party's paper, *The Morning Star*. By this time the paper had long since been made into a co-operative, called the *People's Press Printing Society,* and control handed over to an editor who, it was orally agreed, would be a member of the Party's Executive Committee, or one recommended by them, plus a number of others elected at a meeting of all members of the society. Anyone could join by buying a £1 share. Organisations, such as trade unions, were also encouraged to join. Little care was taken to protect the paper from any hostile takeover, the possibility of which was probably hardly considered.

What had not been considered, either, was the possibility that the editor might become disaffected in some way and use his central position to dissociate the paper from Party policy. And this is precisely what happened. The editor, Tony Chater, a member of the Party EC, had been criticised at a Party conference for the increasing sectarianism of the paper's contents, it was deadly dull and overweighted with trade-union affairs to the detriment of what might be of more general interest to the wider readership we were seeking. The conference made it clear that the majority of comrades wanted a more open approach that would aim to attract this much broader readership. The current circulation was far too small to sustain the paper reliably, which was in financial difficulties and, in any case, the Party itself was developing its policies in a far less sectarian direction.

Tony refused to accept that the paper's contents were responsible for its difficulties and persuaded most of the Management Committee to back him. Meetings were called in a number of large centres, the main one, which I attended, being in London. A long and at times bitter argument ensued, at which the Party leadership tried to get the meeting to replace the existing editor with another comrade. Many of us had come from various areas in the south to support this move. But Chater had been doing some organising of his own and had gathered around himself all those elements in the Party and some influential figures outside it who were dissatisfied with the direction the Party was taking. At the meeting in London, stewards appointed by him were in control of entry to and exit from the hall as they were of the whole proceedings and how they were run. The upshot was that the vote went in his favour and the paper had, by perfectly legal means, been taken out of the hands of the Party. A further meeting merely confirmed the decision of the first one.

We had established the paper, sustained it, often at great financial and personal sacrifice, devoting ourselves to its sale and promotion and now we had lost it! I felt very bitter at this turn of events and even more so when the editor refused to print letters, mine among them, supporting the Party and opposing his actions. A number of comrades then left the Party and formed The Communist Party of Britain which was generally considered to be composed of supporters of the new management of *The Morning Star*. It was no surprise to me when my old comrade, Morrie, joined this new organisation. Both the CPB and the NCP still exist.

What has this lengthy diversion into the Party's internal politics got to do with me, and my story? A great deal. I had devoted my whole adult life to activities based on the belief, which I still hold, that our present system encourages greed, is socially divisive and gives rise to hatred and anti-social behaviour. It is based on the exploitation of one person by another and its central core, profit above all, has led to impoverishment, homelessness (both major causes of crime) and the terrible environmental dangers which the whole world faces today. The struggle for markets and access to natural resources has also given rise to terrible wars which have wiped out millions of people and brought misery to millions of others.

I do not deny that our present system has also led to enormous advances in science and technology which have brought benefits, though some of these are being challenged by Greens today, and an improved standard of living for many, an abundance of consumer goods and durables and that, as a result of bitter and sometimes bloody struggles, a degree of democracy has been achieved in the technically advanced countries.

But the cost of these advantages, especially to the rest of the world where the majority of mankind resides, has been immense, and that they are not sustainable is evidenced by the regular slumps and mass unemployment that I have experienced in my lifetime. And, as to democracy, one has only to cite recent German and Italian history to show how, when their privileges are threatened, the economically powerful in each country will support a strong leader who will not hesitate to destroy the democratic gains I mention, to protect themselves from communists, socialists, trade-unionists and anyone, even the church, who seeks to persuade people of the rottenness of the system.

Like many another young person in the Thirties, angry at the distress and unnecessary misery caused, to myself among millions of others, by this system, I joined the Party which had seemed to show itself as the only organisation really serious in its intention to bring about a world based on ideals of social justice and harmony by putting people's interests before those of personal profit. Productive resources, it insisted, should be utilised only for social purposes, to satisfy the needs of all and for this, those resources ought to be owned and controlled by society as a whole and not privately.

But this did not mean that we campaigned for immediate socialism and neglected the day to day struggle for advances of every kind under the present system. Far from it. We were at the forefront of demands for better pay, improvements in the lot of the unemployed and homeless and general improvement in those services which the state provided for the sick and the coming generation. Some of our members were trade-union leaders, not given to empty rhetoric about the distant future but engaged in hard-headed negotiations for immediate demands. And I was involved in all this activity. So when, after over half a century's membership, with all that it implied, I saw the Party beginning to break up, I was not only deeply emotionally stirred but realised that I had some hard thinking to do. One thing was clear, however, capitalism, with all its inherent iniquities, had not basically changed, despite some considerable modification, and neither had my determination to play a part in bringing about a different, more socially equitable system.

There was intense discussion and a great deal of wrangling going on in the Brighton branch. With the departure of the more sectarian of the comrades to the two new organisations, two more or less opposing factions remained, although the divisions were sometimes not nearly so stark as that may sound. I belonged, I believe, to what I would broadly describe as the mainstream. We recognised many of the faults and mistakes which had been made in the past, some of which arose out of historical circumstances beyond our control, but more often from our own rigidity of thinking. And we determined that there must be changes both as to our methods and direction and this determination was partly behind The British Road to Socialism, which recognised, among other things, that the Soviet path was not for us.

We also saw the need for an opening out towards environmentalism and, especially, feminism, areas to which we had paid lip-service in the past but had neglected in practice. But we saw no value whatever in breast-beating, more particularly as the crimes committed or supported by the major political parties had never been either admitted or publicly regretted. No, as I have already said, capitalism had not changed and hideous results of its core values were still being perpetrated every day. This was not a time to retreat from visions of a fairer society; quite the contrary. The world was more than ever in need of such a vision, as the dangers threatening us all were greater than ever. What was needed was a new approach both to the attainment of and practices within socialism. And this had to be worked out in detail. But to lose faith in the ideal was unthinkable, a capitulation to the dark forces of reaction.

The other tendency within the Party, both nationally and locally, saw the collapse of the socialist countries as evidence of the impossibility of attaining our old ideals in the near, or even the distant future and, as one protagonist put it, they were "not interested in experiments in socialism". They believed that the best we could hope for was "regulated capitalism" and that we should seek the support, based on the widest consultation for such "regulation". They also criticised the Party's whole structure and former methods and wanted a completely new constitution. Oddly enough, the draft of this, to which most of us eventually agreed, still contained the aim of socialism, "which should be green and feminist". But this turned out to be a device for getting approval from all of us with the aim, later, when this faction were in firmer control, to ditch socialism altogether.

The main protagonist for this point of view in our branch was a comrade with a brilliant brain, who was masterly in argument, even when I disagreed with him, which I often did, and had outstanding organisational abilities. He was also the Sussex District organiser of the Party. Because of his intellectual and political prestige within the branch he had considerable influence, as did a number of other political heavyweights in the national sphere, so that their views gained much support, especially among the younger and inexperienced comrades. And especially in view of the collapse of the former socialist states, on whom so much hope and loyalty had been lavished by all of us.

But what all these comrades seemed to lack was a historical perspective, the ability to see what had happened in its historical context. Indeed, they seemed to dismiss such facts if they did not suit their argument.

I once pointed out the development of socialist ideas and beliefs in Britain, through the ages - from John Ball, a leader of the Peasants' Revolt of 1381, right up to William Morris in the 19th century, via the Levellers in the English Revolution, in order to show the continued endurance of these ideas and to predict that they would not die. The comrade I have referred to heaped scorn on this contention by calling it "triumphalism". I noted, however, that he made no attempt to counter my argument.

Politics is a complicated and, at times, frustrating human activity. For me, it engages the mind and the heart and all the emotions. One looks around, one rubs shoulders with others, one experiences, one forms certain conceptions and - above all - one reacts. But politics is not only, and perhaps not mainly, what local or national government does. Politics is concerned with everyday life. If you get the sack and are unemployed, if you cannot afford to rent or buy a decent home, if there is a low level of educational opportunity, if you fall sick and help is slow in coming - that's politics. Or perhaps I should say: what you do about it, what you feel empowered to do is politics. Some people feel impelled to play a part in changing those things that they find unsatisfactory; some don't. The reader will long since have judged to which of these groups I belong!

PERSONAL AND SOCIAL LIFE

When we first came back to Britain in July, I had a job already and could start working in September at the beginning of the term. Rita had still to find employment but, in August, she had obtained a position with the GDR trade delegation in London. This was the nearest thing to an embassy, as the GDR was not recognised by Britain, or any other Western government, at that time; they were all under pressure from the US and West Germany not to do so. She was engaged as a translator by one of the GDR state firms, with an office in Albermarle St. in the West End. So she also started in September and had to commute.

It was a valuable experience for her, enabling her to get a grounding in the trade and technical terminology of the engineering industry. But it also put her in touch with many new English colleagues - good for her mastery of the language and for her understanding of our culture. She also got to know the West End better than I did, my own knowledge having been acquired some forty years earlier when I was working in Regent St.

One of the perks of her job, in which I sometimes shared, was the occasional reception that the firm organised, usually in a large hotel in Park Lane. This was also an opportunity to meet Rita's colleagues as well as some old friends. It should be stressed that the GDR was trying to gain international recognition as a sovereign state, claiming a seat in the United Nations and membership of its affiliated bodies such as the WHO, UNICEF and UNESCO. There were a number of MPs and other notables who were sympathetic to this aim, surprisingly, even a few Tories. Ian Mikardo, the Labour MP, was one of the best known supporters. Such people were usually invited to these affairs.

We began to acquire a circle of friends in Brighton but we also maintained contact with our London friends and, of course, my family. We often invited people from London to visit us and we, in turn, made frequent trips to town. We stayed with my parents and they - and my sisters - got to know Rita, as did the local comrades and friends in Temple Fortune. The Amiels were very hospitable and Rita and I always enjoyed the congenial company we met there. The Borins, too, were especially warmly welcoming and Rita gradually became one of our circle. As a foreigner, feeling her way in a new country among new people, this was particularly important and I know she greatly appreciated the welcome she received from my rather large circle of friends and acquaintances.

Visits abroad were also now on the order of the day. Shortly after we came back to England from the GDR, we had a ten-day visit to Paris, at the invitation of a French colleague I had worked with in Leipzig. His name was Leon Pulvermacher, and his parents had been murdered by the Nazis. He came from Alsace Lorraine and spoke a fluent German. We stayed in their flat and had a whale of a time. It was before Fleur was born and we were footloose and fancy-free. We did all the sights, including, of course, the *Tour Eiffel*. Montmartre was also on our itinerary, as was the Paris opera, where we had the centre seats, in the front row, right behind the conductor. The opera was Carmen and it was quite an experience, watching the singers as they came into view, directing their gaze at him in much the same way that the orchestra does. I'd never realised that before.

With Rita in front of the Eiffel Tower 1966

Later, we went to a night-club with our hosts. Sitting at a table on the edge of the dining area, we felt quite exposed and, as we ought to have expected, when a cabaret artiste was looking for members of the audience to drag onto the stage she made straight for us and yanked me out of my seat. Normally I'm not too shy and, as an experienced amateur actor, have no stage fright, but here I was going to be confronted with a foreign language which I had only half mastered. However, I managed to understand what she wanted me to do and put on something of a show. It got a bit dicey when she called a Frenchman up to play the role of my girlfriend! I learned afterwards that Leon and Mimi were curled up with embarrassment. But I survived, indeed, won considerable applause. A fellow Englishman who was there was heard to murmur: "I wouldn't do that for a million!" One disappointment was when we went to the Louvre and found that the staff were on strike.

We also made regular trips back to Rita's home in Rathen, mentioned above, where we stayed with her parents. In those days we usually drove there in the car, first in the Škoda which I had brought to England with me from the GDR, and later in British cars, until I got a new Lada - but that's a later story. On one occasion we travelled a carefully thought-out route through France, Switzerland and West Germany; a very exciting and fascinating trip, aiming to finish up in Rathen. The trip was not without incident, however.

When changing money in a bank in Chartres, I left my passport behind and only discovered the loss when we arrived at our hostelry many miles distant. In reply to my frenzied 'phone call the bank disclaimed any knowledge of the passport. So I had to report it to the police at Dijon, a long journey, and then proceed, well out of our way, to Lyons, the nearest British consulate. Of course the consul was out when we got there but, luckily, when he returned he issued me with another passport without demur. This may have been because on contacting the Embassy in Paris he had been told that they already knew of my case as the bank had contacted them and reported the incident, a procedure which, I learnt later, is laid down by international protocol.

Soon after we returned home, we discovered that we were about to start a family. Our joy at this news was sadly muted when, just as we were on a visit to my parents, with Rita some five months into her pregnancy, my father collapsed from a heart attack and died in front of our eyes, seated at the kitchen table. A few minutes previously he had asked me if we were going to have the "little finger" (i.e. the baby) circumcised. "How do you know the baby will be a boy?" I asked. Those were the last words we spoke to each other. It saddened me considerably that he had not lived to see his second grandchild, whom I'm sure he would have adored.

On 8 December 1968, our daughter, Fleur, was born, named after the character in Galsworthy's *Forsyte Saga,* whose serialisation on TV, Rita and I had watched with fascination. I had rushed Rita to Brighton General Hospital several days previously and, when I turned up on the following Sunday afternoon, I found her bed empty! Seeing my look of consternation, a kindly woman in the next bed who was having her third said: "Don't worry, young man, she's in the labour room, having your baby". Without a word, I dashed out to get some flowers. When I returned, a nurse was carrying a small bundle in her arms.

I intercepted her and had a good look at my firstborn. All I could see were two enormous blue eyes. I also noticed the tag "Baby Goldman". "You can alter that to Fleur", I said. I didn't know whether to follow her or to enter the labour room. Common sense prevailed and I went in to see Rita. The baby was a few weeks premature, she would have to be in the incubator for a time, more than a week, as it turned out. And when Rita came home with me, we had to leave Fleur behind. This meant regular visits to the hospital until, on Christmas Eve, we were able to bring our baby home to the room which had been prepared for her.

Fleur aged six

145

Despite early problems and inevitable inexperience, we coped remarkably well, at least Rita did because, although I occasionally changed nappies and helped in whatever ways I could, the main burden of childcare fell on her. The very day we brought our baby home, we had a visitor, our friend, the Leipzig Fair agent, Denis Hayes. His visit had been arranged long before. Indeed, he had visited us at Christmas for the last few years and it had become something of a standing event. We debated whether to cancel it, on account of the new and early arrival, but decided to brave it out - we could manage, we told ourselves. And manage we did, despite the fact that I had to take over the cooking arrangements and we ran out of nappies at an awkward moment and the feeding bottle broke.

Of sleepless nights there were many; again, I'm ashamed to say, it was mostly Rita who suffered. The "handicap" of having a baby, however, did not interfere with our continued visits to London. It was on one of these visits that we were both invited to Jeffrey Borin's Barmitzvah. Attending the religious ceremony, Rita got her first taste of gender segregation on the women's balcony at the local synagogue and witnessed the proceedings from there. The reception was held at the Park Lane Hotel and I had to propose two toasts, one to the Barmitzvah boy and the other to his parents, the latter because their brother-in-law, who was to have done the honours, was unwell, so I combined the two. Afterwards a relative remarked in our hearing that it was the best Barmitzvah oration he had ever heard - and I didn't even blush.

At Jeffrey's Barmitzvah

On my return to Brighton I again became a regular supporter of the Albion and for many years I regularly attended their matches. They were soon again down in the Third Division, where I had left them some forty years earlier, having soared to the heights of the then First Division and nearly won the Cup. My physical support at the ground eventually tailed off but they continue to have my moral and emotional support. Indeed, when they were in the First Division and came up against my other ancient love, the Arsenal, I found myself rooting for the Blue-and-Whites and not the Reds! Now that they are entering the first Division, I have high hopes of them.

I had been a strong and passionate swimmer in my youth, swimming in the sea from spring to autumn. But, in the intervening years the sea had become polluted and its delights were less attractive, though I still went in from time to time. One great change I noticed, of course, was the absence of bathing huts - or personal tents - that had once been a seemingly permanent feature of "our" beach. As my swimming gradually petered out I took to fairly regular visits to the Prince Regent, although I had never been keen on fresh-water swimming. In latter years I've become either lazy or at least less enthusiastic and my swimming tends to be confined to visits abroad in warmer climes.

One of my reasons for returning to Brighton after working in the GDR for 7 years, when I could easily have gone back to my old job in London, was that I had certain hopes - one might even say, longings - that I might meet up again with my old schoolteacher, "Wag" Gordon. The thought occasionally crossed my mind in the first years of my return but I did nothing about it. One evening, I was at a meeting of the National Association of Teachers of English (NATE) in a lovely room in a beautiful old house at the end of Eastern Terrace, which was then part of the Teachers' Training College. It was a pleasant convivial meeting and, in conversation with an elderly colleague, I mentioned that I had been a pupil at Christ Church School and had been taught by a Mr. Gordon.

"Bill Gordon," she said, " I knew him well, and Ted Smith, his colleague". I asked her if she could put me in touch with them. She gave me Mr. Smith's address, the only one she knew, and I wrote to him. I ventured, tentatively, that I supposed he had forgotten me but I reminded him that my school nickname was Fatty and told him that I had eventually entered his own profession and even had a university degree. He replied with a lovely letter that I have kept to this day. Yes, he remembered me well, I was the obvious choice for Falstaff that year, he remarked. He gave me Bill Gordon's address. Apparently he (Ted) had become Head of the English Department at Bognor Training College, after the war, and had persuaded Bill to join him. Ted had retired, he was 70 at the time, but Bill, who had married Elizabeth, Head of Maths at the college, was still lecturing.

I wrote, addressing him as "Dear Wag" but he signed his very welcoming reply, "Bill". He invited us to his flat in Bognor for tea and we met his wife, Elizabeth, who served us with delicious home-made scones. He was fatter, of course, which exaggerated his rather short height, something we had never noticed as pupils. He had lost that lean and wiry look by which I remembered him but had gained in poise. I also noticed that he seemed to be somewhat crippled, limping a little on his left leg. I later discovered that it was hip trouble, which an operation some time afterwards seemed to cure.

We reminisced and yarned about old times, perhaps to the boredom of our wives but we quickly established a friendship which lasted to the end of his life. I discovered that he was just eleven years older than me - a lifetime when I was a boy but at this age it hardly mattered. We began to visit each other on a regular basis. His uncle had left him a modernised crofter's cottage in the Cairngorms, at Nethy Bridge, and he asked us to come and stay with them one summer.

We took Fleur, four-and-a-half by this time, and had a marvellous holiday, walking, climbing and even swimming in the "burr-n". Elizabeth's cooking was superb. Bill and I played chess, a game he had taught us at school and at which I did rather well as a boy, but I found that, whilst he had improved, my game had deteriorated and he usually won. Later on, I went to see him at the college where he showed me the model sets which he used to test out the lighting for the drama production he put on there. Elizabeth had helped him with these. She was not only a mathematician but also an excellent amateur jeweller and, even more commendable, a singer of some substance, singing in the cathedral choir at Chichester

Of my former classmates I only ever met two. One was Billy Mountain, an old friend from Christ Church School I hadn't seen him since we were both about 13. Since then we'd reached well into our fifties. I think it was Wag (sorry, Bill) who must have written to Billy, who'd since dropped the y, I discovered, and told him of my recent arrival in Brighton. It seemed that he was now married, with two teenage children and lived in Doncaster but visited Brighton regularly as he loved the place and its childhood memories

I shall call him Billy to distinguish him from Wag (gets confusing doesn't it?). He wrote to me and the next time he came down on holiday he contacted me. I met Rona, his wife and their two children and we resumed our friendship. I noticed that the daughter looked remarkably like Billy as a schoolboy. We saw each other regularly, every time they came down and, on the occasion when I was motoring with Fleur and Rita to Scotland to stay with Bill and Elizabeth, we stopped off at Billy's place and stayed with them for a few days. They entertained us regally. Rona's cooking was heavenly. His health has deteriorated recently and they haven't visited Brighton for some few years but we keep in touch by Christmas card.

The other former classmate that I met again was Bob Black. Bob and I and another chum used to go out over the downs at weekends in the old days, forming a close-knit trio. Bob was brilliant at English and had got an apprenticeship at the Argus as a cub reporter when he left school. I believe that, in later life, he became the proprietor of a provincial paper in the Home Counties. At this time, however, he was back in Brighton in charge of publicity for the town. I was in the information centre looking for some posters to take abroad with me for lectures on Britain that I was going to give in the GDR, when I heard one of the assistants mention Bob Black. Pricking up my ears, I decided to ask to see him.

Soon, a short, stout, very bald man stood before me. But age could not fool me. Bob still blinked incessantly and had long, pointed, artistic fingers, just as I remembered him in youth. He did not recognise me, of course. "Len Goldman", I said. He looked puzzled. "Don't you remember, Fatty Goldman? Light dawned. "But you were such a fat little chap," he said. "Bob", I replied, "I was certainly fat - but never little." We had a short chat. I gave him Bill Gordon's address and suggested that he should get in touch with him. Later I heard from Bill that Bob had visited him and they'd had a convivial evening.

Acutely aware of our responsibility as parents, we had registered Fleur at the White House Nursery School in Ladies' Mile Rd. Patcham at birth and, in the September before her third birthday, she started what was to be a most enjoyable and profitable two years of constructive play and learning. Our forethought had paid off, but the paucity of state Nursery School places in Brighton was a disgrace, with about three such schools for the whole town. It is interesting to recall that, in an effort to bring Fleur up bi-lingual, Rita had always spoken to her in German and this was her major language, although she had also picked up English from me and our friends.

We wondered how she would cope linguistically and were glad that one of the Nursery School teachers could speak some German. We need not have worried about any possible linguistic handicap. She rapidly went over to English but, of course, to the detriment of her German. Fortunately however, constant visits to Germany, where most people she met had no English, meant that she continued to understand and speak the language. Indeed, her pronunciation is probably better than mine.

Fleur began at her first "real" school, Carden Infants, in the September 1973, before her 5th birthday, thus gaining an extra year's schooling, of which, looking back, I feel she took full advantage. Next came the Junior School on the same campus, where I hoped more pressure would be put on her and especially that some homework would be set. In this I was disappointed. There was far too much of the old traditional attitude. Some are high achievers, some are middling and some are poor. We will do our best for them but that's how they come to us and, with a few possible exceptions, that's how they will remain until they leave us. Nature intended it that way. No-one ever used those words but that was how I interpreted the school philosophy.

As my own educational philosophy has previously been described at some length, the reader will realise how strongly I object to that approach. I would also stress that little contact was made with the parents. I cannot recall many events to which parents were invited. I do remember one, however. For purely economic reasons, the school went over to classes of mixed-age groups and we were invited to the school for the Head to explain to us how educationally advantageous this was! I cannot honestly say that Fleur was greatly inspired by her school experiences but the school had a workmanlike atmosphere and she progressed well.

One offshoot of Fleur starting school was that she made many new friends and we began to get to know the other parents. Furthermore, we joined a baby-sitting club and again added to our acquaintanceships. Amongst these were a few families with whom we have kept in close contact ever since - that is, for thirty years. First, there were the Binsteads, Richard and Sheila who, it so happened, was also a colleague of mine at Stringer and their three children. Richard was a journalist, later working at the Argus, from which he has recently retired. Richard was a man of many parts. In addition to his normal work, he had two specialities: music and food, writing pieces about local restaurants and also about concerts and operas. I greatly admired - and envied - his prowess in these two fields. Sad to relate, Sheila died of cancer some years ago.

Another family was the Peasgoods. Fleur was at Junior School with Hilary, and her parents, Adrian and Madeleine, as well as Hilary's two younger brothers, became our friends. This was another fruitful friendship. Adrian was the Librarian at the university and so, as I am passionately devoted to words and literature, we had much in common. Madeleine was also a qualified librarian but eventually became a legal expert. We saw each other's children grow up and have watched their development with interest. We also attended many Town and Gown evenings together, whilst that joint university-and-local-friends organisation still existed.

When Fleur had started at Infant School Rita had been able to seek employment in Brighton. She obtained a post at a branch of Interlingua, a translating agency. This was again a new departure, with texts of every imaginable kind coming in and certain pressures to meet the deadlines. She was now surrounded by a whole new group of colleagues. There was Gerry, the manager, formerly of the Foreign Office, who had worked abroad and had command of several languages, specialising in Dutch. Another colleague was Jim. Of special interest to me, he was a Secondary Modern boy, who was something of a polyglot, his languages including Hebrew! That there were many foreign colleagues, from Asia, South America and Europe, was of great interest and benefit to Rita and, as always, this was also of great benefit to me as we often met on social occasions . Indeed, we retain contact with an Italian lady whose efficient translating skills are still going strong. Later, the Brighton branch shut down and Rita had to travel to the main office in Ashurstwood.

When we first came back to England, I think Rita envisaged it as a rather flat and perhaps not very exciting countryside by comparison with her dramatic fir-clad mountains. In order to disabuse her of this false idea and to give her enjoyable holidays at the same time, I decided to let her see some of our spectacular landscapes. The first and obvious choice was the Lake District, which we visited in my little Škoda. I think Rita was suitably impressed with the grandeur of the scenery, but pushing Fleur up hill and down dale meant that her push-chair was never the same again!

Next came Cornwall. We had a room looking out over the Atlantic in a lovely cottage in Gunwalloe, a delightful seaside village. Our landlady's cooking was superb but - we shan't try lobster again! A visit to Snowdonia now seemed necessary to enlarge if not complete Rita's British topographical education, so the following year we stayed in Dolgellau, and walked up Snowdon with Fleur in her little town shoes. We also visited the famous castles built by Edward I. One very welcome interlude in our Welsh holiday was the visit of our friends from London, Pam Gauntlett and her German husband, Erwin. One evening, we attended a sing-song in the local chapel and tried to sing along with the congregation

In Brighton, two very welcome visitors were Ebs and Albrecht who, on an official trip to English universities, snatched a few free days to come down to Brighton, enabling us to repay them for their unending hospitality in Leipzig. My old colleague from Leipzig days, Arnošt Klimá, professor of History at Prague, was another visitor. Arnošt was a fellow-resident in *Haus der Wissenschaftler* in Leipzig and had been in the resistance during the war. On his 75th birthday his students had produced a *Festschrift* for him, of which he sent me a copy.

Foreign holidays in the early Seventies included Cavtat in Yugoslavia, Majorca, (oh those English pubs), Sorrento, where a visit to Pompeii was a must and we continued to make regular visits back to the GDR to see Rita's family, as well as old friends. In writing this, I am reminded of the wonderful help and hospitality we received from GDR colleagues. In Berlin, we were usually met by Lothar who, with his wife Ipsi, entertained us lavishly. A few days in Leipzig followed, with Ebs and Usch or Albrecht and Doris, whose welcome was genuine and heart-warming.

Rita and I used to do quite a bit of shopping either in Leipzig or Dresden or, nearer home, in the county town of Pirna, where Rita had been to school. We still have some of the excellent wares I bought at that time, including clothing but also household and electrical goods. Children's clothing was particularly good value since all articles for children, including schoolbooks, were heavily subsidised. This is worth mentioning because the impression given over here is of shortages and general shabbiness in the GDR. And there were media stories about how all the factories had to be scrapped after re-unification!. Boringly predictable half-truths.

In Rathen it was always exhilarating to experience the mountains again and watch or travel on the steamers on the Elbe. And of course it was a great pleasure to be with Werner and Gretel once more and enjoy their hospitality. We regaled them with news of our exploits in Brighton and Werner used to question me closely about a whole range of subjects, especially English history. He was very interested in Henry VIII and wanted to know all the details of the wives and what relation this had to the religion and politics of the time. I hope I was up to his interrogation. At least it was good for my German! He knew the area like the back of his hand and was a wonderful guide through the mountains and woods. When Fleur became part of the entourage, it added another dimension to the visits.

Finally, a word about Fleur's transfer to Secondary School. She set her face against going to the school "where Dad taught", so she went to Varndean. By this time, the Comprehensive system was in place, as detailed above, but this did not prevent the children being divided into sheep and goats, as I have also described. Fleur's latent abilities were quite considerable; she worked hard, always completed her homework without any pressure from us and, when she finally took the state examinations, she obtained several good 'O' Levels and some CSEs and was able to go on to further study at the Technical College in her preferred subject, catering and hotel management, a four-year course, at the end of which she obtained her HCIMA.

So, all in all, what with Fleur growing up into a responsible young citizen, pursuing her own agenda and the very varied social and cultural life we led, the whole pattern of our existence had undergone a number of subtle changes. And, of course, we were growing older This did not hinder our trips abroad but increasingly we used the plane instead of the car. Working locally meant that Rita was no longer compelled to spend boring and time-wasting journeys by train and we had all the more time for entertainment and cultural enrichment. Were we mellowing? Others must judge, but we were certainly enjoying life.

In full spate at my retirement celebration 1980

RETIREMENT

The pressures at school and the extra responsibilities I undertook in the union were beginning to take their toll and, as I approached my 64th birthday, I decided on early retirement. I am glad to say that, since the school became Comprehensive, the examination results in History, both 'O' Level and CSE, had been very satisfactory. Colleagues in the department and I were working well as a team and, insofar as exam results are any criterion, and they are certainly not the only one, this had its beneficial effects on the pupils. So it is not surprising that one or two of the latter, in their Fourth Year, when told of my decision, complained bitterly that I was "letting them down". It is true that I was leaving in the middle of their two-year course but that would be true for the Fourth Year whenever I left and, I persuaded them, I was sure that my replacement would steer them successfully through their exams.

The end of term arrived at last and there was some excitement in my tutor group. They were waiting for me to come in and, when I did so, I found two parcels on my desk. I opened one and it contained a lovely set of wine glasses. I set to work on the other which turned out to be a mystery parcel of the kind beloved by schoolchildren. I kept finding other, smaller parcels inside. It took me ages to reach the tiny wrapping in the middle with a small sweet in it. Great amusement from the class - in which I joined and, oh dear, it was now too late for us to go to assembly!

That evening the staff had a party in the small hall, the usual event when colleagues are leaving. As Ruby Besch was also leaving, we had a joint farewell. After thanking us for her present, Ruby spoke about her very interesting career, giving some delightful details of the colleagues she had taught with and children she had taught. As she had accompanied a party of children sent away from home during the war, she was able to describe some hilarious moments.

Then it was my turn. I received a tape-recorder from the staff and an electric drill from the LEA. I began my talk by remarking that I had come to a certain view of life and society at an early age and, through all the vicissitudes

(I remember loving that word!) of life I had not only substantially retained that view but even strengthened it and now held it more strongly than ever. They all knew what I meant. I went on to detail some of my experiences along the way and made reference to my somewhat unusual path into the noble profession. In particular, I mentioned the remarks of a headteacher who had spoken to us would-be teachers, when we were still in the army.

"Remember," he had said," never be frightened of the Head who is only an employee the same as you." This went down well. A colleague was recording my speech because Haydn Passant, the former Head of PE, couldn't be there and wanted a record of what I had said. When saying his personal good-bye previously and wishing me well, Mr. Hodell had told me that I would always be welcome whenever I cared to visit the school. We'd had our educational differences but - we were still colleagues. In his speech of farewell to Ruby and me, he referred to our professionalism which was meant, and understood by us, as high praise.

A handshake from the Head. A dim picture but a brilliant moment.

One of the first fruits of retirement was being able to take a holiday in term time. At the end of September we all went off to Crete. It was a lovely hotel, some few miles from Heraklion and right on the beach. Every morning we got up before breakfast and went for a swim. Passing the open-air pool, I dived in, swam a length and then straight into the sea, which was so clear one could see the sand at the bottom. The temperature stayed at 80 in the shade the whole holiday.

Of course, we travelled into Heraklion and visited the famous palace. What a thrill it was to see in reality the pictures I had so often seen in the history books, especially the Bull Jumpers and the well known sculpting of a bull's head and the remains of the labyrinth that figures in the myth about the Minotaur. Later Greek holidays took us to Rhodes, Samos, Cyprus and the mainland. Before all these trips we tried to acquire a little Greek, first learning the alphabet which word, oddly enough, comes from its first two letters. It was great fun reading every street name, every placard and advert and even bits of the newspaper. Once you know the alphabet it's surprising how many words you can recognise.

One amusing - and profitable - incident arose in Crete because of my small acquaintance with the language. I was looking at the fruit in one of the shops inside the hotel and the owner's little boy had just come home from school, carrying his textbooks. What more natural than that I should ask to look at one. Its title, in Greek, read: *Istoria Ecclesiastica*. "Ah" I said, having read it out in Greek, "the History of the Church". The boy, who obviously knew some English, turned to his father in amazement and told him that this foreigner could speak Greek. Whereupon the man picked out a luscious bunch of grapes and handed them to me as a gift. Never has fruit been more easily earned.

In July 1981, quite out of the blue, we all got a nasty shock. By this time Rita had left Interlingua and obtained a post at Sussex University, in the School of European Studies as a bi-lingual secretary. I often used to go and pick her up, now that I had retired. On this particular day I had driven there, with Fleur, and had just parked the car and was walking towards Rita's office when I suddenly collapsed. I know nothing of what happened but must rely on Fleur's report. Apparently I'd had a heart attack, a cardiac arrest, no less. I tried to rise, stumbled and fell again. She rushed for help. Someone with knowledge of resuscitation was luckily nearby and managed to start the process before the university doctor could get to me with a more advanced apparatus.

A security guard brought in an ambulance with his walkie-talkie (no mobile 'phones in those days) and I was whisked away to the A and E at the Sussex County and placed in intensive care. I'm told I regained consciousness there and even had a personal conversation with a social worker but I can recall nothing of this and, when I woke up again next day, I was in an ordinary ward, and Rita was sitting beside me. Later I was surrounded by friends and colleagues who had been very concerned when they heard the news. Apparently Dr. Chamberlain, the famous heart consultant, had taken personal charge of my case and, all in all, I was a very lucky chap Apart from all the help so fortuitously available, I learnt that the cardiac ambulance was the only one on duty that day as all the others were on strike!

I was greatly warmed by all the letters, telegrams and flowers sent to me by colleagues, family and friends. I particularly remember the telegram from Haydn Passant, which said (I paraphrase): "Some people will do anything to get among those pretty nurses." I remained in hospital for several days and, from looking around, I thanked my lucky stars that I wasn't in the condition of some others in my ward. I had to take it easy on my return home and Rita organised a string of visitors, including two of my sisters from London. Meanwhile, my mother who, although partially sighted, was in a blind home in Surrey, had to be told that my car was under repair when she anxiously enquired why I had stopped visiting her.

With Harold, outside his London hotel 1980

Harold Leventhal had been visiting us again from New York, mainly on music business but he usually spared some time for us and we always enjoyed seeing him. I loved to be reminded of the pleasanter side of our India experiences and the days and nights we spent with our Bengali friends and like-minded servicemen from both our countries.

Nandita, one of the beautiful Chatterjee girls from my time in India, 40 years previously, makes a rare visit to London with her husband.
From the left: Natalie, Harold's wife; Nandita's husband; Nandita; Rita and me.

I was also very interested, of course, in his highly successful music promotion. One of his protegés (I think I can call him that) was Pete Seeger, the internationally famous folk singer and a particular favourite of mine. Harold frequently urged me to come and visit them in New York and promised us, Fleur included, comfortable accommodation in their large flat in Riverside Drive, high above the Hudson River.

In March 1983, a year or two after my heart attack, we decided to take him up on this and, scraping our savings together, we booked our flight to John Kennedy Airport. It was the longest flight we had ever undertaken, 7 hours, and we knew that we faced jet-lag at the end of it, especially as we were flying through the night. Harold met us at the airport and we were driven to his apartment. On the way we glimpsed, with a shock of recognition, the famous Manhattan skyline, with the skyscrapers etched against the morning sky. It was an image we had often seen on the screen, now it was for real. We had to be prepared for a number of new experiences.

The entrance to his imposing block of flats was "commanded" by a uniformed commissionaire who was part of the security arrangements in place in most such buildings. Harold introduced us to him and, as it were," okayed" us with him. We were to be let in without scrutiny. We shot up to their fourteenth-storey flat and were greeted by his wife, Natalie. We had never met any of the family and, for me, it was an emotionally charged moment. He had been a young bachelor when I first knew him, now he had a wife and two grown-up daughters. Natalie made us very welcome and showed us to the flat within a flat that was to be our home for some ten days and where we could be quite private when we wanted to be. There was a lovely view right across to the river.

Our stay was crowded with incident and events. Where to begin? We did all the tourist spots, of course, the Empire State Building, Times Square, Washington Square, Broadway, the Statue of Liberty, glimpsed from across the river, the Museum of Natural History, Bloomingdale's and so on. We also went to the Metropolitan Opera to hear Wagner's *Parsifal.* I found it interminably lengthy and rather boring so we left at the interval, ie after about 4 hours. The memory that stays with me is of the incredible enthusiasm of the New York audience. I have never heard or seen such tumultuous applause, with people on their feet, cheering and clapping wildly and at great length, even after an aria, let alone at the end of an act. A much more enjoyable experience for me was a performance at Radio City, of Gershwin's *Porgy and Bess*, a musical I had never seen in full but whose tunes are known the world over.

The Times Square visit was most interesting. Firstly, there was a large crowd of black youngsters playing, not baseball or American football but soccer, English style. And could they play! There were some really talented players who seemed to me (was it just pleasant surprise?) well up to professional standards. The other side of the coin was the more or less open distribution - against cash - of what appeared to be "joints". A police car drove up, the chap standing next to me quickly put his package down behind a pillar, was searched by the police and - they drove off again but not before they had arrested someone else. I later saw them letting him out of their car. The onlookers showed little interest, they were more interested in the game.

We went out several times with our hosts. On one memorable occasion they drove us all the way to their little cottage in the country, quite some distance away, in Connecticut. There was a small lake in the garden, sometimes visited by snakes they told us, to Fleur's horror. The cottage was actually let, at the time, but they felt the tenant would not mind their showing us round. On the return journey they took us to some friends, old comrades who, like Harold, had long since severed any close connection with the movement but who loved to chat about old times, a pastime to which I was not at all averse.

They also took us out to a meal occasionally and once we treated them to a meal in a Jewish restaurant which seemed to me to be typically American rather than typically Jewish. Maybe it was both. But the outing which was most impressive was when they received an invitation to a meeting on South Africa in the United Nations building and took us along. Simply touring the building was a pleasure in itself. The meeting was also very interesting. I saw, on the leaflet, that an old friend of mine Vella Pillay, a South African of Indian origin, was due to speak. I had met Vella at an International Youth Festival and looked forward to meeting and greeting him in this entirely unexpected way. Unfortunately, he had left by the time we got there.

I cannot pass on from our New York visit without mentioning an unforgettable occasion at Harold's when Pete Seeger spent a night with them on his way to a concert. To cap it all, after supper, he sang to us at the table. The song was his own composition: *Where have all the flowers gone.* What a thrill! Harold also took us to his office once or twice and, on one occasion, we met Paul Robeson junior, the singer's son. I was able to tell him of my acquaintance with his father and we reminisced a little. I got the impression that he did not share his father's political convictions.

Our visit coincided with Pesach (Passover). I was intrigued to discover that they celebrated Seder Night, the first evening of Pesach with a traditional reading from the Haggadah, the book which tells the story of the exodus from Egypt and includes an explanation of the traditional ceremonial acts. The book, like many other Jewish holy books, is usually written in Hebrew on one page with a translation in the national vernacular on the opposite page. They asked me to read from the English text. What memories that evoked. As a boy it had been my lot to ask the *Feer Kashas* (four questions) in front of the whole assembly of family and friends. But in those days I read them in Hebrew. I was later congratulated on my reading; it seems that a cultivated English accent has its admirers across the Atlantic.

We were greatly impressed with the kaleidoscope of New York life: the towering buildings in Manhattan, the glittering shops - and the bag people outside those shops, so-called because all their belongings were in the plastic bags they held on to as they begged, sometimes right outside shops like Gucci's with silk ties in the windows selling at prices that would have kept those bag people in comfort for a week! We were warned not to go to Harlem or travel on the subway. We did both and again saw something of the squalor behind the glitter. I was not surprised as, some years earlier, President Kennedy had told the world that 40 million Americans "go to bed hungry every night." If this is the acme of "modernity" and "the end of history" as Professor Fukuyama claims, then God help us all!

From New York we flew to San Francisco, where we stayed in the Best Western hotel. The Golden Gate, Alcatraz, the little yellow tramway (sorry, streetcar) up the steep hill, China Town, where we encountered a waiter hurrying along the street with a tiny piglet on a silver tray, already sliced and prepared for roasting, the three little symbolic figures in mock ivory we bought there, that still grace our lounge, the Japanese tea gardens; all these things and more are markers of our visit. But the most exciting events were two coach tours we made.

One was to Yosemite National Park, in the romantic Sierra Nevada, where our driver-guide warned us about bears which, of course, we never saw. But the glorious scenery was different from anything I have ever seen. The magnificent waterfalls, alone, make the trip worthwhile. Incidentally, the driver was a most interesting man. An American Israeli, big as a house, who had obviously chosen the sybaritic life in the US instead of Israel's harsh realities. He was a mine of information: geographical, zoological, botanical, historical and so on and so on. And he rolled it forth in a continuous stream throughout the whole journey. During a break, I had a serious chat with him about Israel and its policies and we found ourselves at least partly in agreement.

162

The next trip was to Monterey (*"It happened in Monterey, a long time ago..o..o"*) and Carmel - John Steinbeck country. We stopped at the little canning village, the location for his *Cannery Row*. There was a bust of him and a memorial at the roadside, where Rita took a photo of me and I of her, standing next to this portrayal of the great man. The 7-mile scenic drive has left a thrilling memory.

From San Francisco we flew to Los Angeles and stayed in a Best Western hotel again in Hollywood. There were several purposes to our visit. We wanted to visit a studio and, conveniently, one of Harold's daughters worked for a production company with offices at MGM. On arrival, after a brief 'phone call from the security man to her, we were waved through in the car I had hired. We were met by a young, attractive, dark-haired girl who very efficiently guided us through the studios. Fleur wanted to see the set where *Fame* was made. This turned out to be a rather bare nondescript hall. When we enquired if there were any rehearsals scheduled that we might possibly watch, we were told that the group were touring in England and, at that precise moment were performing - in Brighton! We were presented however, with their latest disc, not yet on sale in the UK.

Fleur was very keen to sample the delights of Disneyland, still a novelty. We spent a whole day there, enjoying the various "rides" and seeing and hearing some fascinating, mechanically controlled puppets: a house of parrots singing catchy tunes, dancing and singing bears and fearsome pirates who shot at us when we went on the river ride. I declined to accompany Fleur on the switchback so Rita had that task and I don't think was that enamoured of the experience.

On the way home, we passed a large hotel where men were laying down a long red carpet in preparation, we later learned, for the Oscar awards which were to take place that very night. Due to the need for New Yorkers to view the ceremony on TV and the several hours time lag, the ceremony started very late. But we stayed up and had a ringside seat in our hotel bedroom. Next day we drove to Malibu beach. It was a cold day and the beach, we discovered, was of very fine shingle, not sand. We walked along the water's edge and watched the sandpipers running backwards and forwards with the movement of the tide. Those sandpipers, and the cold Rita caught as a result of the sharp wind, are the memories of our visit to Malibu.

We flew back to New York, on our way home, fully sated with memories of California. The flight was uneventful but, as we were walking from the plane to the reception hall, we noticed a stunningly attractive but disconsolate lady, whose face seemed familiar, sitting on a chair flanked by two minders. It wasn't? Surely it couldn't be? But it was - the film star, Lisa Minelli, daughter of the even more famous, Judy Garland. Apparently she had left God knows how many thousand dollars worth of fur coat at Los Angeles Airport after the Oscar award ceremony the night before. We 'phoned Harold from the airport to find out about a Paul Robeson memorial concert he had organised at Carnegie Hall. He told me that some of the seats had to be "papered" but the concert was a success. We returned to England, somewhat jet-lagged but a full English breakfast at the airport hotel told our bellies that we were home at last.

One activity I felt able to undertake again, now that I was to have more leisure, was translating from German into English. Luckily, a very well known Leipzig publisher of art history books, *Edition Leipzig,* contacted me and I did two books for them. One of these was: *Dresden wie es die Maler Sahen* (Dresden Through the Artist's Eye) and the other was: *Gartenkunst im Wandel der Zeit* (The Art of Gardening Through the Ages). Apart from the joy of finding the right solutions for a whole host of specialist terms, I also learnt a great deal from the content of these books, as I had to do quite a bit of research to find the English equivalents.

After my retirement, I didn't just fade away and hide myself at home but continued for a few years to do supply teaching in my old school. The pay was not wonderful but it helped the family budget and, more important from my point of view, kept me in touch with education and young people, an interest I shall maintain until my dying day. Indeed, I also continued full membership of my union and remained the Press Secretary of my local association for many years. I became so well acquainted with Radio Brighton (as it then was) that I could have found my way through its corridors blindfold. I still have tapes of several interviews I gave and am proud of the fact that, during the last strike, I was rung up by a member of a rival union and congratulated on the way I presented the teachers' case on the radio.

My replacement as Head of History was Ken Potts, a tall, slim, curly-haired young man, tremendously keen on each student having a file in which they kept their notes and task-sheets. He had enormous nervous energy and always seemed to be seeking something that he couldn't find. When he came into my room after his successful interview, he asked me a few questions but hardly seemed to listen to the answers. Instead, he prowled round the room, as though sniffing at the various pictures and teaching aids I had placed round the walls and cupboards. I learned later, when I came in on supply, that he had trashed all my sets of duplicated notes. His methods were to be vastly different from mine. Fair enough. On one occasion, I had to come in and take over his classes when he was away for a week. An interesting experience.

He left after a couple of years, to become an estate agent, I believe, and John Simkin took over. John turned out to be an exceptionally gifted teacher. Alongside his teaching he ran a publishing house, producing school books, mainly History, of a very high standard, most of which he wrote himself. Just imagine, in addition to a full teaching load and leadership of a department, he researched, wrote and produced these excellent books, some of which are on the shelves in front of me as I write.

John completed several very successful years at Stringer, including being form tutor of the most difficult class in the school one year. I know because, on supply, I'd had to deal with them more than once and it taxed all my skill. As far as I could see, he had them eating out of his hand. They once told him that they felt he "was one of them". He told me he thought that a doubtful tribute! He left, eventually, to concentrate on his research and publishing, ably assisted by Judith, his wife, who also held down a demanding job in the caring profession. We have remained in contact as they live not far from us.

My third successor was Dave Bradley, bright-eyed and full of humour, although I've been told that his constant punning can irritate (a warning to me, here!). Dave, who has recently left, had a wonderful way with the youngsters and was very popular. We met at all school functions - which I regularly attend. I have hardly missed any in the twenty-one years since I left: school plays, orchestral and choir concerts, prize days, leaving celebrations of colleagues who are retiring or moving jobs. I also make a point of appearing at old-scholars reunions, where it gives me great pleasure to meet again and converse with my former pupils and find out what has happened to them since they left the school's tender care. And they seem very happy to tell me.

I certainly made the most of the increased leisure my retirement brought: holidays during term time, a long-desired trip to America, undertaking translation work from abroad again, supply teaching to keep my hand in and enable me to remain educationally involved. It all gave a lift to the spirit that otherwise may have become dull and lifeless. I took a great interest in my successors, so much so that we had a photograph taken together at a school function. And the old scholars reunions are always a delight.

The four heads of History;
From left to right: Myself, Ken, John, Dave.

MY FAMILY

Psychologists are constantly telling us how important family influences are on our character and behaviour, our perceptions and abilities. And I am certainly no exception. My parents, Myer and Janie, were very different from each other. My father's background was not highly educational although his schooling was more advanced than that of any of his siblings. Born in Leeds and brought up in a slum area of Birmingham, where his father's cobbler's shop was in the front room, and by parents whose English was halting and whose mother tongue was Yiddish, his great strength was an extensive vocabulary, a quick wit - he was an inveterate punster! - and an easy, jovial manner. He spoke a fluent Yiddish, too. He was well liked and known to all as friendly and helpful. His interests were football, he remained a supporter of Aston Villa all his life and, in his early years, horse-racing but his interest in gambling waned with the passing years and was confined to playing solo with his friends, at a penny a point!.

He was a simple, more or less apolitical man who read little, was very fond of his wife and children and was never happier than in the midst of his family. When flush, he loved to give us little treats. Not given to deep introspection, he tended to act upon his feelings rather than as the result of carefully thought out logic. He was often worried by financial problems; as a one-man concern his business was always precarious, but when things went well he forgot his troubles and was ready for a laugh at all times. His character and attitudes had their effects on my feelings and ambitions. I didn't get much intellectual stimulus from my father but I believe my gift of the gab was, at any rate partly, due to his fascination with words.

Janie was of a very different stamp. Her father was a rabbi, a learned man, though with a perilously small income; she'd been to *gymnasium* (Grammar School) and was of an intellectual bent. She spoke Yiddish, Russian and a smattering of German, when she arrived here shortly after her sixteenth birthday. Under Myer's guidance, her English soon became fluent, better than most of our foreign friends, but at the cost of her Russian, although she continued to read Russian books and occasionally practiced the language with Russian-speaking friends. She loved reading and often became quite emotional about the sad parts when she recited the story to me, as she often did.

She had been a member of the *Bund*, the Jewish section of the revolutionary movement in Russia and remained a socialist all her life. She always claimed to have influenced my political thinking and (as I remarked in my first book) who am I to argue with that? She largely suppressed her intellectual and artistic longings, in order to devote herself entirely to her family. She insisted on healthy eating long before it became fashionable. We sometimes found this tiresome as she was a very persistent person, indeed.

My mother at 84

She was not, however, the archetypal Jewish matriarch, being much too soft-hearted. One word she used a lot was *nebuch* which, freely translated, means: "poor thing". I think I have inherited some of her sentimentality or, more generously described, sensitive feelings and I know I have imbibed her love of learning. One thing is certain, we all blossomed under her love and devotion. I sometimes wonder if *we* influenced *her*, in any way. At any rate, she joined the Party when already quite elderly.

At 86, a widow, but still able to run a two-storey house with two lodgers, my mother was knocked down at a crossing and injured. Though not fatal, the incident led to a deterioration in her condition and, after a trial period with my youngest sister, she had to be admitted to a home. Dread word! Already only partially sighted, she became registered blind and so it was the Jewish Blind Home in Westcott, near Dorking in Surrey, that agreed to take her in.

My sisters and I visited her regularly and I was usually accompanied by Rita and, sometimes, Fleur. She loved her "Grannie Janie" but was not at all keen on the general atmosphere - and smell - of an old people's home and I must say I don't blame her. We tried to bring some fresh air into my mother's life and engage her in intelligent conversation which, she complained, was sadly lacking from the other inmates. The problem was that it was not only her sight which was defective but her hearing also, making conversation rather difficult.

The matron was German and non-Jewish and one of the assistants was an elderly lady who had survived a concentration camp and still had her camp number tattooed on her wrist. We engaged them both in German conversation and found out a little more about the home. One day, my sister, Etta, 'phoned to say that Janie was seriously ill and we were all to go to the home immediately. When we arrived we found mother asleep and didn't want to wake her. We sat at her bedside and reminisced about our lives. I kissed her but we left without speaking to her. The next call from my sister told me that our mother had died.

It's a sad day when both parents have gone. Mother had devoted her whole life to her children and our sense of loss was deep. We buried her in the Jewish cemetery and I, as the son, had to say *Kaddish* (prayer for the dead) just as I had for my father, buried in the same cemetery. The Hebrew I had learnt for my Barmitzvah was now decidedly rusty but, fortunately, there is help for such ignoramuses as me. A thoughtful source has produced a version of the prayer in English phonetics, so I did not suffer the embarrassment I might otherwise have done. A few months after her death, another sadness intruded on our lives: Rita's father, who had suffered greatly for several months, finally passed away. I had not just lost a father-in-law, I had also lost a good and helpful friend.

My siblings - three sisters - were also all influenced in various ways by our parents and, of course, we influenced each other. I cannot speak for them but I know that having sisters gave me a certain insight into the female psyche if only in a subtle and indirect way. Their friends often became part of our circle and this meant that, with no effort on my part, I became acquainted with a lot of girls and lost the shyness that, *in those days*, afflicted some schoolboys in the presence of the opposite sex. I am unable to say, however, what long-term effects this might have had!

As we got older, the usual sibling squabbles faded into a deep regard for each other. It is with bitter regret that I record that, to the loss of my parents, I must now add the loss of my youngest (Etta) and my eldest sister(Helen), the latter only hours after I penned the above paragraph. They leave a gap in the chain of my life that can not be filled.

Though coming comparatively late, it is obvious that my marriage and the daughter it has produced have been the central factor in my life for the last forty years. Mutuality of interest and support go so deep that their influence is impossible to calculate. Where such emotions are concerned it is better to allow them to seep through one's personality and not to talk too much about them. The birth of a child brings great joy if also new problems and it is certainly fascinating and challenging to take part in the growth of a new human. And the enrichment of our lives is still, after over thirty years, an ongoing process.

Celebrating our Silver Wedding

Whereas previously I had only been a teacher, dishing it out, as soon as Fleur started school, I became a school-visiting parent as well, on the receiving end, so to speak. I'm not sure whether this helped me in dealing with the parents of my pupils but it did make me more acutely aware of the "invisible presence" in the classroom. Children bring more than their breakfast with them into school every morning! One effect of Fleur's attending Varndean was that it gave me an insight into how that school was organised and I was able to assess its impact on my own daughter. Altogether a salutory experience.

In 1988, Fleur finished her HCIMA course and decided to travel abroad for a year before seeking regular employment. She had been working hard in her spare time for some years in order to save money but also to gain experience in her forthcoming profession, "at the sharp end". Now she wanted to go to Australia with Mandy, a fellow student. They intended to travel via the States. We were, of course, rather apprehensive and knew we should miss her. But she had made up her mind, accumulated enough money, kitted herself out, obtained her visa and was ready to start. Now the duties of a father began. I did two things.

First, I got in touch with Harold, in New York, and apprised him of Fleur's imminent arrival on his shores, with her friend. He generously agreed to put them up for their short stay in New York. Next I wrote to a cousin - only recently discovered - who had made his home in Australia. I introduced myself, said a word or two about his mother, my youngest aunt, who had died tragically in a bus accident when he was still an infant, and told him of Fleur's intentions. He also immediately invited Fleur and her friend to stay with them whilst in Melbourne, their first port of call. So all was set. I'd done what I could to ease the early stages of their trip. All that remained was to drive them to the airport. I'd become a family man. It does much for one's ego, on the one hand, but impels you to think of someone else, on the other.

Fleur remained in constant contact with us by 'phone, although the reception was often muffled, and by airmail. So we were able to follow her movements. She intended to maintain herself by doing whatever casual work offered itself. This turned out to be of considerable advantage when she returned to England, because a lot of the work was in catering and, in one place at least, a government canteen, she so impressed the manager that she gave her a wonderful reference which helped when seeking a post over here. Her companion left her, half way through the trip, to return home. But by this time Fleur was well integrated and self-sufficient.

After exactly a year, to the day, she flew back via Hawaii and when we picked her up at Gatwick she was still wearing tropical clothing, shorts and all - and the weather here was freezing! She'd included a six-week tour of New Zealand in her itinerary, had enjoyed the whole experience immensely and brought back a detailed diary with pictures. She had made many friends, one of whom she is still in touch with, as she lives in Brighton! Now that she was back she had to look around for a job. A hotel chain with hotels in Brighton was looking for an assistant manager for their Salisbury hotel. Fleur applied and was appointed.

It was her first real professional post since she had graduated and she was quite excited at the prospect of starting on her career. The job was no great shakes and the manager, a woman, was downright unpleasant. Nonetheless, it was experience which, they say, is cheap at any price. It also had one unexpected result which sealed Fleur's fate. She met Tony. He was installing electrical equipment in the hotel and - he lived in Brighton. To cut a long story short, when Fleur finally gave in her notice and moved back to us, unwilling to tolerate a tyrannical manager any longer, it wasn't long before we were introduced to Tony, a beefy six-footer. They eventually teamed up and have since produced two gorgeous grand-daughters for us.

Fleur and Tony 2000

Yes, my little Fleur, little no longer, is now the mother of two beautiful (I would say that wouldn't I?) little girls, Sasha (4) and Poppy (6) and a lively pair they are, too. Tony is brilliant in arousing and maintaining their interest in their surroundings. It is not sufficient, for example, just to pick up a stone, he must perforce direct their attention to any small fossil that the stone may contain. Nothing is too small or insignificant for him to call their attention to it as part of the wonderful country walks that he and Fleur take them on. Thus their curiosity in the natural world is encouraged and developed - and it shows. Poppy, now at Infant School, keen as mustard to enquire and learn, has already been noticed and praised (proud gran'pa). Sasha, full of mischief and inventive with it, has a natural charm that attracts all who see her. She will never be satisfied with the humdrum. Their talents are varied and complementary.

Fleur in 1994

Apart from his other accomplishments, Tony is also outstandingly practical and artistic with it, and I think the girls, each in their own way, are absorbing both those qualities. And gran'pa, in *his* own way, derives quiet satisfaction from their development and looks forward to the day when they are sufficiently competent at writing to help them, perhaps, in those linguistic skills which he, himself, has always tried to master.

With Poppy and Sasha 2001

When Sasha was on the way, it became apparent that, if Fleur was to retain her post as manager of the catering unit at a prestigious local girls' college, after her statutory period of leave, we were going to have to help

173

with the new baby. As Rita was on the point of retiring from her post as translator with patent attorneys, she would be available to give the necessary assistance. Sasha arrived (large blue eyes and golden hair) and Rita retired and again, as with Poppy, took on the responsibilities associated with looking after a small baby. Hard work - yes: nerve-wracking at times - yes, but what a joy, too. It was mainly Rita upon whom the burden fell, I'm far less adept, though I gave back-up where I could. Now that they are both at school, we are freer and can go on holiday when it suits *us*.

Perhaps I should round off this part of the story by quoting the last three stanzas of a little verse I composed, greeting a group of friends at a garden party to celebrate my 20 years of retirement. After describing every guest, in some detail, without actually naming them, I came to my own family - all present - and this was how it went:

My sweetheart, always at my side,
There's Fleur and Tony, too,
Who've filled us with deserved pride
Presenting us with two

Cherubic rascals, gorgeous imps,
With smiles and laughter wild,
Which you must watch to catch a glimpse
Of the individual child.

With such a tribe, yes, who can doubt
That I'm a happy gent;
To those who'll listen I can shout:
"That's what my life has meant!"

RETIREMENT - WHAT RETIREMENT?

My interest in what's going on in the world - locally, nationally and internationally - has never waned. Retirement was but an opportunity to devote more time to political and social activities. In short, I may have retired from my professional job, but not from life. There are so many aspects to the quest for social justice and peace in the world.

I had been a member of the Great Britain-GDR Society ever since I returned from the GDR. Now that I had more time, I decided to volunteer to be its secretary in Brighton (later extended to Sussex). I organised meetings, film shows and socials of various kinds at which I either spoke myself or, with luck, dragooned a visiting GDR personality to come and answer questions. I also gave lectures to many other groups: Labour Party and trade-union branches, co-op guilds, other political and social organisations, schools and colleges. Very often, these talks followed a visit back home with Rita, when I usually managed to meet a wide variety of GDR people and glean much about the situation there.

I was always scrupulously careful to give a balanced account, giving equal weight to the negative and to the positive sides of life there - and I still have my notes to prove it. One of these talks was to an after-school group at Lancing College. It was early in 1990, shortly before reunification of Germany. After the discussion, which was lively and contentious, I received a letter from one of the staff who had been present. He was probably anti-GDR, but warmly appreciative of my lecture , although he seemed somehow disappointed that I had been too even-handed in my approach. I just didn't conform to the stereotypical Leftie who would sugar-coat everything in the GDR. That just wasn't my pitch.

Towards the end of the Eighties, there were ominous, or exciting, depending on your point of view, signs of political change both on the Left, locally and nationally, as well as in the socialist countries. The attempted coup against Gorbachev, in the Soviet Union and its aftermath, with the rise of Yeltsin and the "reforms" he introduced, which led to the eventual collapse of the system; similar developments in the other countries allied to the SU; the effects of all this on those in the West who in one way or another had looked to the "socialist world" for inspiration; all these events came crowding in to influence an already politically volatile situation for the Left in the capitalist world.

Of special interest to me, of course, was what was happening in "Germany", that is between the German Federal Republic, occupying some three-quarters of the original area of the country and with a proportionate population and, on the other hand, the German Democratic Republic in the eastern quarter. A reading of my previous remarks will have given you a rough picture of the economic, political and social problems faced by the latter. In 1989, the GDR was celebrating its fortieth anniversary. Erich Honecker made the usual speech about its achievements, some of them were very real, as I have explained, but the writing was already on the wall (no witty reference intended!).

I wrote a letter to the Guardian that autumn which, by some miracle, they printed, commenting on the situation. In it, I pointed out that a West German takeover was not the only alternative to support for the existing regime and that the population were against reunification, an estimate that was correct at that time, according to a poll taken by a Western journal. In a nutshell, I demanded to know if the best answer to a Press dominated by the leaders of the ruling party, the SED, was a Press dominated by Springer, the West German "Murdoch".

It wasn't capitalism, I argued, that the people wanted but a different form of socialism, the social advances they already enjoyed but without the ubiquitous hardline political control and the restrictions that implied. They were, of course, also impressed with the far greater availability of consumer goods in the West. However, they certainly didn't want mass unemployment, homelessness and the other negative features of capitalism.

Discontent had shown itself in the peaceful street marches that autumn, marches that some of my friends took part in. The demand was for more openness, less surveillance and more freedom of speech etc. It was also clear that the SU, in other words, Gorbachev, having urged changes which were not forthcoming, had withdrawn its support for the ruling group. Waiting in the wings, like hungry wolves (to mix the metaphor) were the West German authorities who whipped up the crowds that began to gather on their side of The Berlin Wall. Overruled by the majority on the Politbureau, the top leadership were unable to declare a state of emergency and order the police to use force, so people marched through the checkpoint in the Wall and freedom of movement in both directions was established.

This freedom was used by various forces in the West, including the neo-nazi *Republikaner,* to march through with banners and slogans, already prepared, proclaiming *their* demands. These latter also declared their intention to recruit in the East. In contrast to the reasonable demands of the GDR protesters, some of the West's banners demanded the return of those former German areas ceded to Poland by the Allies at the end of the war, a demand which, if insisted on, could easily have sparked a third World War. And, in general, with the GDR leadership now in disarray, the West increasingly took charge and, in the campaign leading up to the referendum on reunification, poured in massive quantities of free gifts, especially of goods in short supply in the GDR and flagrantly interfered in the whole process. Shades of Eatanswill, Dickens' hilarious description of a rigged election!

The result - and all that flowed from it - is history and I shall only refer to it insofar as it affected my family and me. The whole period is called *die Wende* in German, meaning the turning point or the big change and it did, indeed, drastically change people's lives over there. Many of my friends and some relatives either lost their jobs or were demoted or blocked from promotion because they had been "too friendly" to the old regime. One internationally known professor was prevented from becoming a "full" professor whilst a former student of his, whose academic achievements were trifling by comparison, was promoted above his head!

Thus, in a thousand ways, the "victors" took their revenge. But - you could certainly buy Mars bars and Western cars were readily available and much cheaper. More important, it was now possible to travel to the West, an opportunity which Rita's relatives and some of my friends could now take advantage of and it was with delight that we were able to welcome several of them in our own home for the first time, an opportunity to repay them for their hospitality to us. Sadly, Rita's parents were not alive to take advantage of this new opportunity but, fortunately, they were able to visit us in GDR times. Her father had died in 1984 and her mother came over on her own once or twice after that until she, too, passed away in 1987, two years before *Die Wende.*

Martin Richter and his son, Roland, have visited and so have Rita's cousins. And Ebs and Albrecht, this time with Doris, have been able to come over on their own steam, so to speak, without having to represent their university, as in the past. So there have certainly been some considerable gains as a result of the changes. Time alone will enable us to draw up a balance sheet. But it is true to say that the euphoria occasioned by the destruction of The Wall has long since been replaced with a more sober assessment.

The effects of all these events on the Left in Britain - and here in Brighton too - have been deep-seated and lasting. As I have explained, there was much soul-searching and even bitter argument in the Party, certainly from the time of the Khrushchev revelations onwards. We had been closely associated with the SU and the other socialist countries, had defended them with our woefully small voice against their very loud-mouthed and powerful enemies and had suffered ostracism in certain quarters and various other impediments to a tranquil and successful life as a result. Was this to be the end of our hopes and dreams?

I felt that many comrades in our local branch were allowing breast-beating (mea culpa; mea culpa) to take over from sober analysis. Yes, we had been wrong not to look more closely at what was happening in the SU et al and to put all negative reports down to hostile propaganda. But their demise was not only due to their own weaknesses and sins. Their policies, including Stalin's brutality, had to be seen in their historical context: the enormous power of their enemies to subvert and eventually destroy them; the crippling cost of "keeping up their guard" holding back their economic development. It should not be forgotten that, in a capitalist country, war and armament are hugely profitable - for some - whilst in a socialist country nobody benefits, everyone loses.

Whilst none of this excuses, it begins to explain why this first socialist "experiment" came to such a catastrophic end. And that's the point for those of us who are still determined to change society from its present basis of individual profit and greed, at no matter whose expense, to one basing itself on the needs of the whole of the community. Historically such a society has been called socialism. You can use a different word if you like.

But, as I have indicated, many former comrades had given up on the idea, either because of the collapse of what had previously been their ideal and the acme of their aims and that, therefore, there was no longer "a model" of socialism and the best we could hope for was regulated capitalism -

178

reformism in other words. They also maintained that the main oppression in our society was no longer, or perhaps never had been, class oppression. Rather it was male chauvinism or racism and any attempt to link this with the social system was pooh-poohed or condemned as " economism" or some such simplification. This was supposed to be New Thinking (note the capital letters) and I have since taken to referring to those engaged in it as New Thinkers.

The interesting thing was that these New Thinkers, those who most strenuously espoused this viewpoint, were often those who had been the most sectarian and hardline in the past. I believe their rejection of "old" ideas, ie socialism, stemmed from an inner need to purge themselves and atone for their former "naivety". I found myself in ideological conflict with many of these comrades who, nonetheless, still remained my friends. I could not accept what I saw as their pessimistic defeatism based on a perfectly natural disappointment. Matters eventually came to a head at a conference called to discuss a completely new constitution and a change of name.

Those who wanted to retain the word "socialist" or possibly "communist" in the name were in a considerable majority as shown by the results of a questionnaire sent to the whole membership. I, for instance, was in favour of calling it The Party of Democratic Socialism. But the New Thinkers were now in control of the machinery of the Party and were able to divide this opposition to their plans to drop either of these words by separating out the various names which included it as though they were in opposing camps, whilst unifying, under one name, all those who agreed with them. The result was that their preferred name: The Democratic Left, won the day.

As a concession to those who retained their belief in socialism, and in order to get their support for the new constitution, it included socialism as our aim and added, uncontroversially, that it should be "green" and "feminist". That this was just a ploy was revealed a year or two later, when, with the New Thinkers now firmly in control, of the whole Party apparatus, including its property and finances, they dropped the term altogether from the constitution. Later still, the name was changed twice, first to The New Times Network and then to The New Politics Network.

This new organisation had long ceased to be a political party. Instead, it was to be a "catalyst for change" and its members could join any party of their choice as long as they agreed with the "aims", all of which, I may say, were quite acceptable to me and, indeed, to any progressive person. Their defect was that they implied that justice, equality and freedom for all could be attained under capitalism, though they did not exclude socialism at some remotely distant date. But any talk of, or propaganda in favour of changing the system was deemed to be a hindrance to the struggle for immediate improvements under the existing system.

In my view, all previous experience shows that the two are not only not contradictory but complementary and have always gone hand in hand. The early, 19th century Marxists, for example, had fought like mad for shorter hours, better working conditions etc whilst pointing out the need for more radical social change. The Democratic Left, both locally and nationally, organised many very useful meetings on various issues and gave valuable help to others engaged in specific activities. Many national speakers were glad to avail themselves of their services in providing ready-made audiences - and footing the bill. One policy which they along with others, strenuously and successfully pursued and in which I participated, was the tactical voting campaign, which deprived the Tories of many a seat in constituencies where the majority didn't want them but were divided.

We in the Brighton (now Sussex) branch, which still calls itself Democratic Left, were and are a lively bunch. We have taken part, again with others, in election campaigns, for the Labour Party in Brighton and the Lib. Dems. in Lewes, and have had many very interesting meetings, with LP and Green Party reps and conducted frequent debates amongst ourselves, with at least two New Thinkers in our midst to add spice to the discussions. The branch meetings are almost invariably held in the home of John and Janet Richards, two comrades who have become close friends of ours.

They are a fascinating couple: he is Public School, scion of an affluent upper-class family and she comes from the working class and - they complement each other perfectly. Their home is one of the most welcoming I know, whether for political or social meetings and parties or for a more personal visit. On all these foregoing occasions the atmosphere is always congenial, they spread that aura however contentious the debate may be. Janet with her affectionate and motherly presence, John laid-back, somewhat amused, debonair, very knowledgeable but always tolerant. It is a background to all our activities which could not be bettered. Rita and I like them so much we've been away on holiday with them on a couple of occasions.

Then there is Peter Avis, a doyen of the British Press. Peter is chairperson of the group and it is to his remarkable skill - and wit - that we largely owe the success of our gatherings. He has a succinct way of summing up to the satisfaction of all. I have not always agreed with him but my admiration for his breadth of knowledge and linguistic skills is unbounded. Some years ago, Peter was on the platform at a broad-based meeting which the Party had helped to organise - on housing I think it was - and after his contribution a colleague sitting next to me whispered some very complimentary remarks about his speech. I swelled with pride. "He's one of us", I whispered back.

At the Great Dieppe Trip 1999. Francis Tonks (L) and other friends

Peter is bilingual in French-English and his other claim to fame is the quite remarkable tradition he has established by organising an annual trip to Dieppe - the Great Dieppe Trip as we call it. It started some twenty years ago and has been going strong, stronger and stronger, in fact, ever since. It began as a one-day, one-off affair and developed into a regular annual weekend. The Dieppe council had been under left-wing leadership since the war and our party of Leftists always got a wonderful, semi-official, welcome with a reception at the town hall, followed by celebratory feasts on other days. The mayoralty has recently gone over to the Gaullists, but that's another story.

181

From Dieppe, we usually visit some other outlying township and are often met by local worthies there. On one memorable occasion we went to Paris to attend the *L'Humanité* festival. It was very exciting but, unfortunately, at the end of the visit I blotted my copybook pretty comprehensively so I shall draw a veil over the whole affair! One of the very enjoyable side-effects of "Le Trip" is that one meets old comrades, some from London, that one doesn't see the rest of the year and local comrades that one normally only meets at official gatherings. Among these are a number of local councillors, regular "Trippers", two of whom have recently become MPs.

I have been retired for over twenty years and now, in my old age (dotage?) I have taken to writing what I think of as witty verse though some have used other epithets. I had honed my poetic skills over the whole of our nearly 40 years of married life by penning a few verses to Rita on the occasions of our wedding anniversary and her birthday. It seems to me that she appreciates this very much and has kept them all, I suppose they must amount to nearly 80 by now. But there was a special occasion on which I started to pen these little ditties for a more public audience. It happened like this.

We were to celebrate the 90th birthday of a local comrade, Eric Scott, journalist and long-distance traveller who had been a reporter on a local paper and, later, on the Daily Worker. Rita and I could not attend as we were committed elsewhere, so I thought I'd write some verses in his honour, entitled: *Great Scott*. Apparently Peter Avis read it out at the party and, on my return, he 'phoned me and reported that the poem "had wowed them". With encouragement like that, I could hardly resist the temptation to further versification.

The next event that moved me to poesy was a social organised by John and Janet. I wrote them a little tribute. This time I was there in person to render it myself. It went down well and they appreciated it. I believe they still have it stuck up in their kitchen. There followed a paean of praise for Peter, called *Peter the Great*. On the occasion of the twentieth anniversary of The Trip, I composed one charting its history from the very first voyage and describing various events and people and enjoyments along the way. Each trip since has had its special poem, read out at the final feast.

Other ditties have invited friends to our garden parties (to which some of them have replied in kind!), congratulated German friends on their "round-number" birthdays. Two, at least, have dwelt on friendship and its wider benefits. Joe and Julia McGirr each received one on their retirement. I also indulge my penchant for verbal juxtaposition by composing on-the-spot limericks about my companions.

We do not neglect cultural pursuits, which are an important part of our lives. I am particularly addicted to the theatre and Rita to opera and our love of orchestral music may be taken for granted. Fortunately Brighton is blessed with many opportunities to enjoy all three of these experiences, especially during our renowned Festival, when some of the world's finest artistes grace our stages and concert halls. We visit the Theatre Royal whenever there is anything worthwhile on there and, more recently, other venues which have been developed including the Pavilion Theatre and the Komedia. And, of course, one should not omit the Gardner Centre at the university where, among many other things, we have seen some excellent Brecht and, on one unforgettable evening, a performance comparing Brecht with Kipling. Just imagine: *Mack the Knife* and *The Road to Mandalay*! Brecht the communist and Kipling the imperialist and yet - surprise, surprise - there's a great deal more common ground between them than one might suppose.

On a trip to London

We are regular attendants at Brighton Philharmonic Society concerts, where some exciting talent has performed with them as soloists. And the New Year concerts at the Dome are a treat not to be missed, always finishing with the rousing Radetzky March, to which the audience clap along. Our favourite opera venue is Glyndebourne when the Touring Company performs, especially since the re-organisation has produced such fine and comfortable viewing and listening from anywhere in the auditorium. But we've also heard excellent opera in the Dome and at the Theatre Royal. We travel to London from time to time to see ballet and opera.

I joined the amateur company that occupies my old school, the New Venture Theatre, in Bedford Place, but so far I haven't had the courage to audition for a part. I'd love to, but fear I wouldn't have the time to attend rehearsals. Every year we go to at least one show at the Chichester Festival Theatre on a trip organised by my old friend and colleague, Peter Stockbridge. Peter began adult life as an actor, switched to teaching after the war and then, after early retirement, returned to acting and has been an outstanding success. He's a few years younger than me but we buoy each other up by defying the ageing process.

Apart from my membership of Democratic Left, as described above, there are many other activities that fill my pensioned days. I work as a volunteer at the Peace and Environment Centre in Gardner St. one day a week (come in and see me some time) where my experience in my youth as a shop assistant stands me in good stead. I must seem ancient to some of my co-workers there, who are a dedicated bunch of youngsters. There are a few older ones, too, but none of my vintage. The centre was set up by the Quakers, CND and a number of other groups.

I work in the well-stocked shop which apart from promoting goods and literature produced by the various organisations we aim to help, FoE T-shirts for instance, also generates some income to back our activities. A fairly new introduction is Fair Trade goods: tea, coffee, etc. These are produced by workers who are guaranteed a proper price and decent working conditions The books mainly relate to environmental and conservation issues. There are also children's books about young people in other lands, how they live, what they eat and wear, their education and how their families gain a living. They have kindly stocked my books, too and have sold quite a lot!

Unfortunately the nuclear-bomb question has taken something of a back seat since the "end of the Cold War", as the movement has been lulled into a false sense of security. But the issue is still alive and, until recently, the anti-nuclear-sub group under the leadership of Duncan Blinkhorn, took their inflatables up to Holy Loch to intercept these subs and raise national consciousness of the dangers to peace and the environment they posed. After decades of such courageous activity, Duncan finally left the Centre for other work. His going was a great loss. He was a young man of tremendous verve and determination and was a pivotal force at the Centre. He has not been replaced as such, but a group of young people share the supervisory work between them.

In the recent Afghanistan crisis we helped to organise vigils for peace at various places, including the Clock Tower and the Memorial in Pavilion Parade. There is also a One World Library and Education Unit which aims to service Brighton schools, in particular about the Third World, runs workshops for teachers and publishes educational research There is a wealth of literature on the environment, sustainable development, peace and security, human rights and much else. For a nominal sum anyone may join and it's well worth it if you are interested in questions of peace, social justice and the environment. An IT centre in the building is now also available to the public and has become very popular. So there's plenty going on there.

I also do a weekly stint on Wednesdays at the Brighthelm Centre. This is a purpose-built building run by the United Free Churches. It houses office accommodation on every floor, occupied by various social organisations, several meeting rooms and a hall, used as a church on Sundays, a small chapel, and a restaurant - and that's where I come in. I serve behind the counter: hot and cold drinks, sandwiches, confectionery, scones, cakes and fruit and I take the money, having first mastered the techniques of a modern cash register. Open to the public, its prices are well below those charged in commercial restaurants.

The customers are mainly pensioners, elderly church-goers and people with various handicaps. The chapel is available for quiet meditation and prayers during the day. What am I - an atheist - doing, helping a church organisation? Simple. I feel the centre is doing a fine job and that's why I support it with what spare time I have, even if I differ from them, to some extent, ideologically. Though it is worth saying that there is a great deal in true Christianity that appeals to a socialist.

I have been a member of CND almost from the beginning, am also in the United Nations Association, have rattled a UNICEF collecting box outside Sainsbury's in London Rd. for several years and I support their meetings and other activities. We play our part in trying to prevent wars, big or small, to restrict the damage they do once they have started and put forward detailed policies for bringing them to a speedy end. The struggle to outlaw nuclear weapons and protect the planet from other deadly dangers is a continuous and arduous one, especially in view of the enormous resources controlled by reactionary forces leading in the opposite direction as against our movement's greatly smaller resources. That is why I feel that my own actions, small and insignificant in themselves, are most effective when united with those of others. The pen - and the spoken word - can be mightier than the sword.

I am also an active member of the local Pensioners' Association, which campaigns for a return to the principle of linking pensions with current earnings, a principle introduced by a Labour Government, rescinded by the Tories, when in office and not (yet!) re-introduced by the present government. That old stalwart, Barbara Castle, is on our side as is another former Labour Movement leader, Jack Jones. We've demonstrated outside party conferences, marched along the sea-front with banners and bands and written letters to the Press and our MPs. I also attend meetings of the Better Government for Older People set up by the council as part of a government initiative - but we haven't seen much movement yet!

From time to time, in my advancing years, I toyed casually with the thought of writing my life story. Looking back, however, I feel it was never a serious intention. "I'm far too lazy," I thought. But I reckoned without Michael. Mike, my former pupil whom I have mentioned above and in the acknowledgements, urged me, more and more insistently, to attempt an autobiography. He already knew something of my life, thought it would interest others and pricked my conscience into activity. I should say that, having left school with no paper qualifications (rather like me, actually!) he had gone on to acquire very good GCEs at 'O' and 'A' Levels at evening classes and had become active in QueenSpark Books where he was chair of the Manuscript Group, ie those who decided which MS to publish from the many submitted.

We are fortunate in Brighton in having QSB, which is non-profitmaking and a thriving member of The Federation of Worker Writers and Community Publishers. It aims to publish the life stories of local people and has already produced nearly 100 titles. The organisation arose in 1972 in a typically British way, during the course of a struggle to prevent the establishment of a casino in Queens Park, one of Brighton's "lungs" and a leisure area much appreciated by local people, especially children. One of the "weapons" used was a street newspaper with a column devoted to residents' memoirs. This encouraged a local man, Albert Paul, to write his life's story, *Poverty, Hardship but Happiness,* which they published as a book, and QSB was born.

Now nearly thirty years old, it is the longest surviving publisher of its kind in the south-east. Its members are greatly varied as to age and background and its slogan is: "Everyone has a story." It runs courses in every aspect of its work: writing groups, a bookmaking group, a manuscript group, a marketing group and so on. It has also operated in schools to encourage children to speak and write about their lives. Apart from the income generated by the books, it gets help from South-east Arts and the local council. I have recently started to become active in the organisation, myself. If you're interested, why not join in?

To return to my own situation, after much hesitation, I decided to accede to Mike's urgings and try my hand. Thus one might say that, as I had helped and encouraged Michael with his schoolboy literary efforts, he now - as it were - returned the compliment. I had quite a good typewriter and started out boldly, tapping away, in duplicate. I had never done anything of this nature before but I was helped by my command of a fair fluency of expression and, surprisingly, a remarkable memory of events and people in the distant past and even what my parents had told me of my very early days. What a contrast to my short-term memory!

After I had produced the first fifty or so pages, Rita suggested that this was perhaps the moment when we ought to take the plunge and buy a computer. The year, I believe, was 1995 and, although computer techniques were already being taught at school, the PC was not nearly so ubiquitous or as well developed as it is today. I was, of course, totally computer illiterate.

So it was with some trepidation that I set about the task of learning the alphabet, so to speak. And I was approaching my eightieth birthday! Fortunately my colleague, Bob Hoare, the computer expert at school who lives quite near, expressed his willingness to help me set the whole thing up and start my education.

Due to his generous assistance and the time he was prepared to spend with a somewhat inept pupil, I managed to get going using this new medium. A further spurt was given to my rather faltering start when Adrian Peasgood, seeing my new acquisition when he visited us, promptly offered to come round and give me a series of lessons. He was brimful of confidence, having recently made a thorough study of the technique when, as Librarian, he'd had computers installed at the university. He told me I was to 'phone him with any further queries that arose. I was also remarkably fortunate that Chris Jones lives just round the corner. His mastery of IT is consummate and I cannot begin to describe the enormous technical help he has unstintingly given me. There have certainly been situations with the last two books where I could not possibly have continued without his unfailing help. It is friends like these who lift my spirits when I feel depressed about computer problems.

Mike had also mastered the computer, indeed, he had one at home, and his wife, to whom I am ever grateful, transferred (ie re-typed) my first 50 pages of MS onto a floppy disc which I was then able to transfer to my machine. Thus I was fully computerised and, despite many panicky moments, I was on my way. I consulted family and friends, did a bit of elementary research and some cursory editing and, when the first draft was finished, I submitted it to QueenSpark. Mike was no longer active there and, after a long delay, the MS was returned - and rejected. It needed thorough editing and they just didn't have the manpower. And that was that.

"OK," I thought, "I'll publish it myself." This meant that there were other new skills to be learnt and other help to be sought before the whole project could be finalised. Editing, for one. I went through the whole thing with a fine toothcomb, looking for typing errors, changing the position of passages, altering words and phrases and so on. Then Rita had a go. She found many more mistakes and made many useful textual suggestions. Then Mike went through it and I made further modifications after a discussion with him. It was then that Julia McGirr generously offered to do a thorough edit.

I am eternally indebted to her for the highly professional job she did. It altered my concept of essentials and enabled me to produce a far better product, although, of course, I take full responsibility for the final version. Now it was necessary for the MS to be prepared for printing. This is where Mike came in again. He set it up on his more advanced PC, transferred the whole to Pagemaker, arranged the text in such a way that there was space for the pictures and that chapters began at the top of the page and so on. Finally, Tony designed a very artistic front cover for me. The whole project had taken me the best part of two years!

I also wanted to register the book and give it an ISBN number. This involves despatching five copies to the various national libraries and to the British Library. The registration is free - apart from the postage. When all this was done and the title pages set up and the Table of Contents and the acknowledgements set out, Mike introduced me to the printer's that QSB had used, *Digaprint*, and I was able to choose from a number of colours for the cover.

Once the book was produced, I had to publicise and sell it. Here, my experience as a commercial salesman stood me in good stead. I asked for and got reviews of the book, a small one in The Argus and a very generous and lengthy one, half a page with large pictures, from Pat Moorman in The Leader, after a very interesting interview. Several other publications and bulletins were kind enough to give the book a mention and I have also given radio interviews, so that when I introduced myself and the book to the booksellers I only got one refusal, the Royal Pavilion bookshop!

Even the small bookshops and one outstanding newsagent, Salmon's of Patcham Village, all co-operated, the latter proving one of my best customers. The next book was easier, as I could start straight away with the computer, making notes and headings first and then systematically going through and developing each theme. A computer makes the printing technicalities much simpler, too, as supplying the printer with a floppy disc of the whole text greatly reduces the cost of printing. It must be obvious that I didn't start the project to make money. I simply wanted, if possible, to cover my printing costs and any other expenses. I have been able to do this, as the books have sold pretty well and I have, as an additional bonus, made many fascinating contacts. People, some of them from my past life, have written and 'phoned, asking for copies and indicating the reasons for their interest I look forward to a similar modest success with this, the final volume.

A LIFE

So what does it all amount to? I am into my eighty-sixth year and what, if anything, have I achieved? I have many friends, both in Britain and abroad and enjoy a rich social and cultural life. I have a wonderful family and have already expressed my feelings about them. But, above all, I am a political animal. At an early age, whilst still at school in fact, I developed a strong sense of justice - and injustice, not only on a personal level but, much more, within the wider, social sphere. I grew up during the depression. Despite an underlying economic insecurity, my family were all sufficiently clothed, fed and housed but I was acutely aware of what was happening elsewhere: the mass unemployment, the widespread ill-health and unhappiness due to poverty. But I was also confronted, in Brighton especially, with conspicuous wealth.

I read of the terrible waste of produce and resources that contrasted with the hardship of millions of fellow-humans, even in the rich countries like Britain and America. I had school friends who came up with answers. I was about thirteen and they were not much older. We may not have been completely clear about all the issues or, still less, of the precise solutions. But we started out on the path that might lead to social justice, as many of our fellow-Briton's have done in the preceding centuries. What a trail of adventure and misadventure I have had since then, of blissful happiness contrasted with black despair and deep dissatisfaction, of wonderful social and personal experience and periods of extreme loneliness.

I have travelled the world, seen almost every European country, as well as Africa, India, Burma and Malaya and made a brief but impressive sojourn across the Atlantic. I've been a shop-assistant, a commercial traveller, a door-to-door canvasser, a soldier, reaching the dizzying heights of sergeant and, finally, a teacher. I showed some ability and had some success in commercial life but, in the end, found it distasteful. I both enjoyed and hated the army (explain that if you can). And as a teacher? Here the verdict has to be much more complicated. I think I have helped to open up horizons for some youngsters, made friends with not a few, failed miserably with many others. Past pupils always seem to have time to chat when we meet.

None of the above is a sufficient appraisal of my life if it ignores my constant and continuing perseverance, despite all the odds, to give my emotional, spiritual and physical energies to what an old Russian writer called "the finest cause in the world - the liberation of mankind". Pompous words with little practical meaning? Or, as I prefer to believe and, whilst I live shall go on believing, the only thing which, in the end, makes life worth living. I fling back in the faces of the pessimists the idea that man is only selfish, greedy and always corruptible, although I concede that we human beings are often all three.

We have another side though, and one meets it every day and in every situation. It is the conditions of life and experience which will always determine whether the negative or positive in our species will dominate. In a grab-all society the responses are obvious and predictable - "there is no such thing as society". How right she was, about the system *she* espoused and gloried in. But our present set-up, although *basically* as it was when I was a boy, has evolved, is part of historical change. It wasn't always thus and the lesson of history is that it will not remain so if we decide to change it. We humans can and will devise a different way of ordering our lives and our relations with nature and each other and our material and spiritual needs, despite the failure of crude first attempts.

It is this belief in a better, more humane future for mankind that has kept me going and still, in the second half of my ninth decade, keeps my spirits high - and I am certain that I am not alone!

Family reunion, with Rita's aunts, cousins and their spouses.

Gran'pa the clown